HANNAH COWLEY

TIVERTON'S PLAYWRIGHT
AND PIONEER FEMINIST
(1743-1809)

Mary de la Mahotiere

DEVON
BOOKS

First published in Great Britain in 1997

British Library Cataloguing in Publication Data

A CIP record for this book is available from the British Library

ISBN 086114 916 5

DEVON BOOKS
Official Publisher to Devon County Council
Halsgrove House
Lower Moor Way
Tiverton Devon EX16 6SS
Tel: 01884 243242
Fax: 01884 243325

The author and publisher acknowledge the generous
support provided by The Heathcoat Trust towards
the publication of this work.

*The cover pictures show Tiverton Castle c. 1800 from a painting by
Rev. John Swete (courtesy Devon Record Office); inset is a portrait of
Hannah Cowley by the miniaturist Richard Cosway RA.*

Printed in Great Britain by BPC Information Ltd, Exeter

Dedication

To all those who have championed
the cause of freedom for women
by word or deed

Hannah Cowley
Pencil drawing on paper, Richard Cosway R.A.
Henry E. Huntington Library and Art Gallery

CONTENTS

ACKNOWLEDGEMENTS

Starting from scratch in 1990, it was difficult to get to know Hannah Cowley really well and my sincerest thanks go to all who helped me in the search:

Professor Frederick Link, Emeritus Professor of English, Nebraska University who sent me xeroxed copies of all the plays; Dr Gretchen Foster, University of Michigan, co-author of *The 'Other' 18th Century: English Women of Letters 1660-1800* who gave me a copy and visited Tiverton in search of Hannah Cowley; Ms Joyce East, Director of Humanities Program at West Virginia Graduate College Institute WV who also came in search; Brown University, Providence RI, for assistance and newsletters of the 'Women Writers' Project'; Henry E. Huntington Library and Art Gallery, San Marino CA, for a copy of the Cosway drawing of Hannah Cowley; Richard Ryder for the picture of Lady Harrowby and the armorial bearings of Nathaniel Ryder..

The Harrowby Trust, Sandon Hall, Staffordshire, which holds 25 volumes of correspondence between the Ryder family and constituents of Tiverton; Chawton House, Alton, Hampshire, the Lerner Foundation for the Study of Early English Women's Writing and publishers of the periodical, *The Female Spectator*; the University of Exeter and Tiverton Library, for access to the papers and books of Genest and the Rev. Mr Chalk; Tiverton Museum, for access to papers and safe-keeping of the broken fragment of Hannah Cowley's tombstone; Gerald Barnett for permission to quote from *Richard and Maria Cosway*, (West Country Books, 1995) and Claire Tomalin for the quotation from *Mrs Jordan's Profession*, (Penguin).

All who have replied to letters of enquiry including the British Library, Fitzwilliam Museum, Cambridge, Royal Commission on Historical Manuscripts, the Garrick Club. All who have listened with interest to talks on Hannah Cowley, the Devonshire Association, the Tiverton Civic Society, the University of the Third Age, and so encouraged publication.

PREFACE

IN SEARCH OF HANNAH COWLEY

It was in 1990, when researching my book on *Tiverton and the Exe Valley*, that I first met with Hannah Cowley. The information leaflet at St George's Church near the Town Hall, Tiverton said:

'A number of interesting persons are commemorated in the churchyard, notably the Rev. Samuel Wesley, Headmaster of Blundell's School (brother of the more well-known John and Charles) and also Hannah Cowley an eighteenth century playwright of some repute'.

I was curious. I was born and chiefly educated in Tiverton but had never heard of a locally-born playwright, least of all a woman playwright. I went in search of her tombstone and found 'Samuel Wesley', let into the eastern wall, but nowhere could I discover 'Hannah Cowley'. I spoke to the verger who told me 'Oh that! When we built the extension, a lot of them had to go'. He was referring to a new hall built on to the back of the Church in 1969. There was no record of what had been removed.

Disconsolate, I sauntered into the nearby Library and asked for the *Dictionary of National Biography*; there I found 'COWLEY (HANNAH), see also Anna Matilda, pseu.', followed by no less than three columns detailing editions of her plays, over sixty editions of the various plays; her poems, some written under the pen name of Anna Matilda were also listed at length. The Library had no other information so I walked down to the Museum, adjoining the Church and struck lucky. The kindly curator was sure they had a fragment of her tombstone somewhere; it proved to be in a locked store and there it stood, a broken reminder of Tiverton's playwright 'of some repute'.

As detailed in the *DNB*, there had been many editions of her plays at home and abroad and, most recently, a two-volume edition (1979) by Garland Publishing Inc. which, unhappily, had gone out of print in 1988. Finally, I was able to obtain copies of this from the editor,

Professor Frederick M. Link, Head of English Studies at the University of Nebraska. It did not surprise me to learn of the interest of Nebraska University, and later of that of Michigan, as Hannah's manuscripts are in the libraries of Yale and Harvard.

At last, thanks to the kindness of Professor Link, I could read the plays and, as I suspected, discovered that Hannah was very much more than a playwright 'of some repute'. From 1776, when her first play, 'The Runaway', took London by storm, until 1794 when her last, 'The Town Before You', signalled her disillusionment with the contemporary London stage where knockabout farce was taking over, she was one of the foremost dramatists of the period.

The most important discovery, however, was that Hannah, the 'unknown' from Tiverton, was one of the very first, if not the first, of true and effective feminists. That does not mean that Hannah would ever have become involved in what are loosely called today 'sex-wars'; quite the reverse. She looked upon marriage as the ideal, a happy union of minds as well as bodies. What she did do, and this was her important contribution to 'fair-dos' for women, was expose and demonstrate in the plays an outrageous injustice. Young women, whether daughters or wards, were mere chattels, entirely at the disposal of their father or guardian who could legally give them in marriage to the highest bidder or to satisfy a personal ambition (improved social status, a title, or access to a Parliamentary seat which would come with the right deal).

Hannah did not rail against this monstrous wrong. She was much more subtle but the plays make the evil effects of arranged marriages all too clear. Two contemporaries of hers are well-known champions of women's rights; Hannah More (1745-1833) and Mary Wollstonecraft ('A Vindication of the Rights of Women', 1792). Their influence has been recognised by all upholders of fair play for women but Hannah delivered her message in a much more powerful medium, the stage. This way, too, it reached everyone from the pit and gallery to the aristocrats in the boxes; in an age when very many people would have been unable to read the arguments in the 'Vindication', this was important.

Audiences in London and provincial theatres, Bath, Dublin, Hull, York, Richmond etc. and audiences in Germany and America could not ignore the desperate effects of this abuse. Most of the plays are fast-moving comedies so the message is never boring; not all were set in England for women were 'chattels' in most countries. Hannah wanted to see freedom of choice, for women not to be the hapless victims of harsh anti-women attitudes based on outmoded customs. Undoubtedly, she was a major contributor to the groundswell of public opinion calling for freedom and independence, although this was not to make itself effectively heard and become incorporated into new legislation until the next century.

I
A PIONEER FEMINIST

The story of Hannah Cowley as a playwright and of how she took the London stage by storm started in 1775 when she and her husband, Thomas, were at the theatre in London at a rather dull play, 'The School for Wives'. 'I could do better than that myself ', she confided to him and he laughed indulgently. The other version of her inspiration says that she asked one of her party what money the author was likely to receive from the piece and the reply 'About five hundred guineas', spurred her to instant action.

In less than three weeks she had written a play, 'The Runaway', that was to run and run, make a tidy sum of money, and, importantly, open people's eyes to the intolerable injustice of arranged marriages. Unsure of its reception, Hannah sent it anonymously to David Garrick, then nearing the end of his phenomenal career. He spared no pains in tracking down the author and put on her play at the Theatre Royal, Drury Lane on 15th February 1776.

THE RUNAWAY - A 'SMASH HIT'

The 'Runaway' is the lovely eighteen-year-old Emily Morley who has had the courage to abscond from the wardship of her uncle who is determined to see her marry a certain Baldwin. She not only does not like Baldwin but finds him positively distasteful, 'His person is ungraceful, his manner assuming and his mind effeminate'. The local kindly and upright landowner, Mr Drummond, discovers her in great distress at a widow's cottage on his estate and brings her to his friend, Mr Hargrave who has a son, George, just down from Oxford for the long vacation, a daughter, Harriet, and a lively niece, Bella, who will be more congenial companions for Emily.

At the Hargrave residence, young George recognises Emily as a girl he had met and fallen in love with at a masked ball but who had then disappeared. She had had the same reaction; they are hopelessly in love. However, there is a complication. George's ambitious father, a widower, has invited into Hargrave Place a fifty-year-old widow, Lady Dinah who, with the blessing of Mr Hargrave, is hell-bent on marrying the personable young son of the house. His father explains to George, 'Oh, she's clever - she's an Earl's sister too, and a forty thousand pounder, boy' adding 'If one could keep her in the family, I say - would not that be a stroke'. Later, we learn that the £40,000 would just enable Hargrave to buy the nearby Greenwood estate and 'we shall then have more land than any family in the country, and a Borough of our own into the bargain'. Not unnaturally, George thinks that it is his father who will bring off this apparently very desirable match. So, convinced that his father himself wants to marry Lady Dinah, George agrees to back it and tells Lady Dinah that he approves; it is a brilliant scene, a classic 'equivoque' or misunderstanding, with George expressing his agreement in well-bred diplomatic nothings leaving Lady Dinah amazed at the lack of passion shown by her husband-to-be. She puts it down to his infatuation with the newly-arrived Emily.

Soon Lady Dinah shows her true colours; she encourages her maid Susan and a man-servant Jarvis to plot against Emily pretending that Jarvis had known her when they were both strolling players (which would confer about as much respectability in the eyes of an established county family as New Age travellers would today). Emily is handicapped because, owing to the disgrace she has brought on her family name, she has refused to reveal it. It looks as if they will succeed in blackening Emily's name and showing that she is nothing but an adventuress bent on infiltrating the Hargrave household in search of a rich husband.

Mr Hargrave's friend, the Justice, an all-too-typical magistrate of the time will hold a court to decide the matter there and then. Things look black for Emily; she has been given to understand that George will marry Lady Dinah, she cannot clear her name without involving the good name of the family. There is nothing for it; in despair she has sent for her guardian, her Uncle Morley. He is indeed 'deus ex machina' - except that he arrives in a coach-and-six. When the venal Justice hears of such affluence, he does a complete *volte-face* and the two servants' plot is revealed, but Uncle Morley insists on taking Emily back to the hated Baldwin immediately and will see she marries him the next day. He is adamant; his niece is guilty of 'stubbornness, wilfulness and ingratitude' and ought to be made to repent, as long as she lives. Now she can never hope to be the wife of another and should snap Baldwin while she can - moreover he has five thousand a year! He will not listen to her pleading, he will not delay, 'you shall be tied fast to Baldwin'.

George, however, will not be cheated of his whole life's happiness, he borrows a chaise and pursues the coach-and-six intending to rescue Emily and take her to France where they can live on what money he has of his own. He succeeds in intercepting the coach, but, unfortunately, Emily has fainted and has been taken to Mr Drummond's house.

Meanwhile, Mr Hargrave had discovered through the servants that Lady Dinah had herself played a disgraceful part in the plot to denounce and get rid of Emily; she had instigated it and moreover had refused to pay Susan and Jarvis the promised reward of £200 for their accusations. When taxed with it, Lady Dinah leaves in high dudgeon complaining that she should never have mixed with 'plebeians'. Emily returns from Mr Drummond's and she and George declare their mutual love and plead with Uncle Morley who, learning that Drummond, who had been a friend of Emily's late father, Major Morley, whole-heartedly approves of the match, gives it his blessing.

The sub-plot in which Harriet, the daughter, had been deterred from declaring her love for young Sir Charles, a friend of George's, has also been cleared up when George and Bella confess they had only pretended Sir Charles was really in love with someone else because they were afraid the reticence of both the young lovers would lead to stalemate and parting unless they were precipitated into revealing their true feelings.

So, two weddings will take place, but this is a young household and there is still the attractive and witty young cousin, Bella, who has played a pole part in the action. So when it is announced that the friend she loves, Belville, had landed at Dover and is on his way to Hargrave Place, the kindly Mr Drummond exclaims 'Then we'll have the three weddings celebrated on the same day'. This, however, does not meet with Bella's approval - 'Oh mercy! - I won't hear of it - 'Love' one might manage that perhaps - but 'honour, obey' - 'tis strange the Ladies had never interest enough to get this ungallant form mended'. Bella's outspoken protest against the marriage vow, 'to love, honour and obey till death do us part' has been earnestly debated and amended ever since, particularly before royal weddings.

There speaks the voice of Hannah Cowley herself; marriage is not to mean the complete suppression of all independent opinion and action.

'All London' flocked to the Theatre Royal, to boxes (Garrick had done away with seats actually on stage), gallery and pit. 'The Runaway' was a 'smash hit' - a 'runaway' success! Comments in *The London Stage* - 'very great applause' and the *Westminster Magazine* - 'a great success' were contemporary tributes; it was the talk of the town, condemned by men in coffee houses and clubs, the 'in' topic of conversation in polite drawing rooms, a by-word with the 'plebs' of the pit. They revelled in seeing the Justice revealed in his true colours (too busy to be bothered with granting licences to inns or approving applications from poor widows and children for Poor Relief, he was instantly stirred to action when told that a poor cottager had taken a hare - typical; prepared to back the two servants' plot against poor Emily so that he would gain the 'favour' of pretty maid Susan, he back-tracked hurriedly when Emily's guardian proved to be a rich man in a coach-and-six). They loved it.

The brilliant cast certainly contributed to the play's success; it included 'Gentleman' Smith as George, William Parsons as the Justice, and in the quieter role of courageous Emily, Sarah Siddons. She was just 21, and a member of the famous Kemble acting family; she had been all the rage in Bath, and Garrick invited her to Drury Lane in 1775 and cast her in 'The Runaway' in 1776. Mrs Siddons left the London scene to go on tour but after her return in 1782 she was the acknowledged 'Queen of Drury Lane'.

Tiverton in the early nineteenth century.

II
THE TIVERTON
BACKGROUND

W
ho was this new unknown playwright? Hannah was born in 1743 to Philip Parkhouse (1712-1790), Tiverton's first bookseller; he had been educated at the renowned West Country grammar school, Blundell's, founded in 1604 by wealthy clothier, Peter Blundell, for local boys, though 'foreigners' might be allowed in to make up numbers. This meant that besides the Day Boys there were many sons of leading county families who had sent their boys as boarders which ensured a wider 'mix' (as well as leading to ongoing friction between the 'free' Day Boys and paying boarders, described in the opening pages of *Lorna Doone*).[1] Besides the study of the classics and Holy

Old Blundell's School where Philip Parkhouse was educated.

Scriptures, verse composition in Latin and Greek was taught and 'spouting' – the art of declamation or oratory. Many pupils would go on to Oxford and Cambridge and the Church. Philip was destined for a Church career until 'family circumstances' made this impossible. Instead, he opened a bookshop in Fore Street, the main thoroughfare for travellers entering the town over the Exe Bridge. It was very convenient for the Town House where the Mayor and Corporation met (Philip was to become a Corporator – 'councillor' in modern terms). Much of the political life of the town took place not in the Council Chamber but in three inns, the Angel which had an underground passageway into the Town House, the Three Tuns (later to be renamed The Lord Palmerston in honour of Tiverton's famous M.P. and Prime Minister) and the White Horse where Fairfax and Cromwell were both said to have stayed during the Civil War.

Philip's mother, up at Barnstaple, was first cousin and friend of John Gay, the exuberant author of 'The Beggar's Opera'. This could account for some of Hannah's flair for playwriting but more important would have been the influence of her father who had married Miss Hannah Richards in 1742.

He doted on his clever and lively daughter and passed on to her all the learning he had acquired at Blundell's besides making real to her the treasures that lay within the covers of the books which crowded his shelves. Very important to her was her father's position in the town as an Assistant Corporator; this meant that he was at the very hub of local politics, at the heart of all the intrigues, gossip and events, hilarious and otherwise which marked out Tiverton as 'one of the rottenest boroughs in England' in the words of Devon historian, W. G. Hoskins.

The unique system of Parliamentary election in Tiverton dated from 1615 when King James, highly displeased with Tiverton's habit of burning itself to the ground (fires of 1598 and 1612), granted a Royal Charter 'for better ordering and government of the same town'.[2] The Charter decreed that Tiverton should elect two members to Parliament and that the right to elect should be vested in 12 Capital Burgesses and

12 Assistant Burgesses (the burgesses were more commonly known as 'corporators') and the Mayor. This meant that any man who could command the votes of thirteen members of the corporation could command two Parliamentary seats[3] with all the access to privilege, public office and patronage that that brought with it. Moreover, Tiverton Corporation was self-perpetuating; 'on the death or resignation of a Capital Burgess, his successor was chosen from among the Assistant Burgesses; on the death, resignation or promotion of an Assistant Burgess, the new corporator was chosen from among the families of close connections of the Corporation.'[3] Every election, every vacancy brought with it bribery of one sort or another, intrigue and double-dealing. And Philip Parkhouse was right in the thick of it (an Assistant Burgess 1774-1776) and could confide in his wife and young Hannah the day-to-day, hour-to-hour goings-on. This 'soap opera' of Town House affairs has, fortunately, survived in the political memoranda of Beavis Wood, Town Clerk from 1768-1798, who reported regularly to his M. P. paymasters, the Ryder family. Philip Parkhouse stands out clearly from a self-seeking and quarrelsome bunch of corporators as 'a sound man among lame brothers'.[4] This friendship between her father and Beavis Wood was to be of great value to Hannah who clearly knew Nathaniel Ryder (created 1st Baron Harrowby in 1776) well; her father was able to ask Tiverton's Member of Parliament to help her financially and her husband too, which he did.

Still more important was the connection with every level of society of the time; Thomas Davies in his 'Memoirs of Garrick' 1808 reviewing Hannah's connection with Garrick writes 'Her knowledge of manners in high life is as exact as if she had lived with people of rank from her infancy'. Her plays, from the very first show complete mastery of the behaviour and language of aristocrats - in 'The Runaway', Lady Dinah and the Justice - and the 'plebs', Susan and Jarvis. Life in a Tiverton bookshop proved an excellent apprenticeship for a playwright; and her next play 'Who's the Dupe?' first performed in April 1779 at Drury Lane, a fast-moving and hilarious farce again dealing with a threatened arranged marriage, shows a shrewd awareness of the state of education.

For a long time, it was impossible to find out anything about Thomas Cowley, Hannah's husband. Clearly the information given by the Victorian F. J. Snell in *Chronicles of Twyford* is incorrect. He states 'Miss Parkhouse married above her station, her bridegroom being Captain Cowley of the East India Service'; this is demonstrably not true, since Thomas Cowley's preferment from a lowly position in the Stamp Office to a commission in the East India Company is described in detail in letters from the Town Clerk of Tiverton and Philip Parkhouse himself to the M.P. who was able to engineer it, Lord Harrowby. Moreover, it is clear that Hannah's achievements as a leading playwright were largely responsible for her husband's career advancement. F. J. Snell can also be discounted for his scathing assessment of Hannah's work; 'although her fame was ephemeral, the admiration of her contemporaries must have been very flattering to her feminine vanity, especially as she could not know that her fame was ephemeral - that she was 'wearing but the garland of a day'. Her plays were still being produced successfully in London and elsewhere during the lifetime of Snell and some are today in America and hopefully, some may be revived in England.

At last, I came across an entry for 1783 in *The Gentleman's Magazine*. Under 'Deaths of Eminent Persons' there was mentioned: 'Mrs Mary Cowley. At Cockermouth, in an advanced age, many years a bookseller in that place and mother-in-law of Mrs Cowley, the dramatic writer'.[5]

The *Cumberland Pacquet*, of June 1783 confirms this. It seems that Thomas was baptised at All Saints, Cockermouth on 7 December 1744 (although the mother's name is not given, this was not at all unusual at the time; Cowley was, too, an uncommon name locally). How did the young couple meet? As both were involved in the bookselling trade, a reasonable surmise would be that books and writing brought them together. The place of marriage is not known to the Devon Record Office; the date is given by Harding in *History of Tiverton* as 1772. It was fortunate that Hannah did meet Thomas; the field of choice of a husband would have been very limited for her in Georgian Tiverton; the local 'corporators' and businessmen were not noted for their intelligence or their conduct but chiefly for being self-serving, opinionated and quarrelsome.

III
WHO'S THE DUPE?
1779 Drury Lane

his hilarious farce was one of Hannah's most successful and long-lasting plays. In the next century, a publisher's note (1813) relates 'This farce has been constantly before the public since its first appearance in 1779 at Drury Lane. It suggested itself to the author's mind on reading a passage in which a sneer at the Inferiority of Women was carried to excess.' The sneer was probably made by an academic, bent on belittling the intellectual abilities of women, for in her Prologue Hannah explains that her play is an answer to:

> *... Learned Men - your Writers,*
> *Whom no age ever mark'd for Fighters;*
> *But war with Women they could wage*
> *And fill their bold, satyric page*
> *With petty foibles - Ladies faults -*
> *Who still endure their rude assaults;*
> *For even now it is the way*
> *In this our polish'd modern day,*
> *On Female Follies to be witty,*
> *From the Court Beauty to the City.*

Hannah asks if she may, in turn, have leave 'To laugh at those same learned Men'. The figure she has chosen is Gradus, a pompous product from 'Brazen- nose' College, Oxford who speaks in the rarefied language of the cloisters peppered with classical allusions which no-one understands.

The rich but uneducated Doiley is determined that his lively only daughter, Elizabeth, shall marry a 'Man of Larning' and who better than

Gradus so clever that the College-heads can't decide whether he should be a 'great Judge, a larned Physician or a Civility Doctor'? Doiley will settle some £50,000 on his daughter because in giving him an erudite son-in-law she will have made up for his disappointment that she was only a girl. 'I was grieved, grieved to the soul, Betty, when thou wert born. I had set my heart upon a boy. If thou'd'st been a Boy, thou shoud'st have had Greek and Algebra and Jometry enough for an Archbishop'. Poor Doiley was brought up in a Charity School and all his money had never compensated for his lack of learning, pitifully he recounts how he lost his chance to become Lord Mayor of London. Three times he was called upon to speak; each time he was too overcome to utter a word and was laughed at and nicknamed 'Dummy'. His lack of education is evident throughout the play; if he can mispronounce a word, he does (a masculine Mrs Malaprop), if he can muddle things, he does (he speaks of Gradus observing the moon 'through a microscope').

Yet Doiley truly loves his daughter and, provided he can have his whim and see her married to a 'Man of Larning', all will be well. Elizabeth, however, is in love with a Captain Granger and has sent for him urgently. Disguised as Elizabeth's dressmaker, Mrs Taffety, he is able to make some telling comments in 'franglais' when Gradus comes in to start his courtship in heavy academic style well-larded with classical allusions which no-one understands; 'Lady, I have more satisfaction in beholding you, than I should have in conversing with Graevius and Gronovius'. Elizabeth points out that 'unfortunately, I don't know the Gentlemen you mentioned. The education given to Women shuts us entirely from such refined acquaintance'. To this Gradus answers, 'Perfectly right, Madam, perfectly right. The charms of Women were never more power-ful - never inspired such achievements, as in those immortal periods, when they could neither read, nor write'. He continues in this vein; he is a monumental bore and at last Elizabeth loses patience and advises him to throw his books into the fire, hire a dancing-master and grow agreeable.

Gradus realises he cannot hope to win Elizabeth as he is and accepts the offer of Elizabeth's cousin, Charlotte, to introduce him to Mr Sandford

(Granger's friend) who will put him right on current social conventions. She explains, 'Knowledge, as you manage it is a downright Bore' and he doesn't even understand the word 'bore' and when she explains further, 'Why, sir, Bore is all the ton', again he is at a loss. When he has mastered such essential words which are 'the short-hand of conversation and convey whole sentiments at once – all one likes is ton and all one hates is bore' and when he has exchanged his grizzle wig and dingy brown coat for something *à la mode*, he'll stand a chance. He will put himself in her hands.

Yes, a complete transformation takes place. When next Gradus appears, he is well-dressed and well-primed to avoid College 'cant', though he does have one or two relapses. When Doiley sees him in his new persona, he is amazed. Gradus is declaring 'Learning, a vile bore' and 'I have no study now but the ton' even 'Learning, I abjure for ever'. Sandford confesses that he couldn't bear to see Elizabeth 'tied to a collection of Greek and Latin quotations' and so had decided to take Gradus in hand and 'English' him. Doiley is furious - 'English 'im'! In doing that he would ruin Doiley's ambition to get an erudite son-in-law. Now is Sandford's chance to mention that he happens to know of Sir Wilford Granger's son who is a great worry to his family because he spends all his time reading Greek and Latin authors and mastering the English philosophers. He promises to try to induce Granger to marry Elizabeth, although he's not too sure he can succeed because neither beauty nor gold has charms for this Granger - 'Knowledge - knowledge is his mistress.'

Doiley is impressed by Granger when he turns up but he is no fool and will have things his own way; he will confront Gradus and Granger and put them to the test to see which is the most larnèd - ha ha!, the winner to get Elizabeth and the fortune. Gradus scents victory and invites Granger to choose his weapons - Hebrew - Greek - Latin - or English. But Doiley rules out English - too common - they are to start off with Greek.

Greek! Poor Granger! Poor Elizabeth! They are undone. Gradus starts off in great style with an epigram in Greek; it contains the word 'panta' four times in two short lines and Doiley is disappointed: 'Panta, tri pantry - Why, that's all about the Pantry'. He is clearly unimpressed; but what can Granger do? He has no Greek; he prevaricates, hoping to find a way out and he has a brainwave; using the initiative that marks the true soldier, he invents and declaims a hotchpotch of English words which would be obscure to Doiley (and many other people). 'Yon lucid orb, in aether pensile ...Chrysalic spheroids th'horizon vivify, astifarious constellation, nocturnal sporades, in refrangerated radii, illume our orb terene'. Doiley is spellbound and invites Gradus to beat that. Gradus protests 'You have heard a rant in English' which serves only to enrage Doiley: 'English - d'ye take me for a fool? D'ye think I don't know my own mother-tongue?' He declares that Granger has won the strange 'trial by gobbledegook'.

Thanks to Granger's brilliant improvisation, Elizabeth is saved from the deadly Gradus and can marry and take her fortune to Granger; Doiley is happy, he has obviously got a scholarly son-in-law; but 'Who is the Dupe?'. Is it Doiley? After all, Granger is hardly a 'man of Learning'. Or is it Gradus? - he didn't get a fair and equal combat. But all ends well - even Gradus is rewarded; cousin Charlotte has taken a liking to him and will help him to read the world instead of books at 'Brazennose'.

So Hannah Cowley has done it again. She has shown that man-made marriages can be ridiculous. Right in the forefront of public perception is the dilemma of Elizabeth who so narrowly escapes the fate of being married against her will to the most boring of academics; and in the course of the plot, Hannah had made her point about women's education. She herself, of course, had, most unusually, had almost the same education as a boy; her father had studied the full academic syllabus at Blundell's and passed it on to Hannah. It was he who composed the Greek epigram which Gradus so proudly delivers. The farce moves at so fast a pace that, watching it, the message could be missed, but it is implicit and absorbed subliminally; much more effectively put across in the play than in the written admonitions of Hannah More and the blue-stocking brigade.

IV
A SERIOUS SET-BACK
Plagiarism and back-stage politics:
Garrick, Sheridan and Hannah More

I t was Garrick who had recognised the merit and profit-making poten-
tial of 'The Runaway' which 'was one of the most profitable plays, both
to the author and manager, that appears on the records of the treasury-
books at each house': Hannah, in the Preface to 'Albina' was referring to
Drury Lane (where Garrick had just decided to leave the stage and had
sold his share of the management to Sheridan) and to the Theatre Royal,
Covent Garden where the manager was Mr Harris. It was clear that
Sheridan, basking in the success of 'The Rivals', 1775 did not welcome
the arrival of a new, wildly popular woman rival. He immediately
'shelf'd' Hannah's play which was not played again that year 'but by
command of their Majesties and for the benefit of performers'. Hannah
confessed, in a letter to Lady Harrowby of 31 October 1777, that her
vanity was piqued but explains:[6]

> Mr Sheridan is too full of himself to pay attention to other authors
> ... That Mr Sheridan is my enemy from principle, I have too much
> reason to believe for he not only last year did all in his power to
> crush 'The Runaway' but this year when Mr Henderson is very
> desirous of performing George Hargrave which he avows to be his
> favourite character and that he had been requested to do by some
> persons of rank who saw him in it frequently at Bath – he is not
> allowed to appear in it; doubtless because it would give the
> comedy a new run and its unfortunate author new reputation'.

Hannah had written a tragedy, 'Albina', before 'Who's The Dupe"; she
was anxious to have it produced for a tragedy was then considered a

Mrs Ryder, afterwards Lady Harrowby.
From a painting by Sir Joshua Reynolds.

higher genre than comedy so it would add to her reputation. When, however, she received no reply to a letter she had sent to Sheridan asking him why 'The Runaway' had been taken off, she decided to send 'Albina' to Mr Harris of the Theatre Royal, Covent Garden. She felt slighted. After several weeks of anxious anticipation, it was returned; Mr Harris maintained that the play was unfit for the stage and that no alteration could ever make it so. Hannah explains to Lady Harrowby:[6]

> the league of friendship established between Mr Sheridan and Mr Harris is fatal to me – each making a point not to accept any piece which the other has refused. This unnatural conjunction between the Managers of the opposite Houses seems to promise ruin for all but one or two established authors, whom they dare not offend.

Hannah had had high hopes for 'Albina' which she had dedicated to Lord Harrowby who had clearly read the play carefully. Hannah had acknowledged his help in a letter of 27 My 1777:[7]

> Indeed, my Lord, I have most zealously endeavoured to obviate all your objections. I believe there is not more than a word, with the reprobating mark, that I have endeavoured to keep in ... A passage in a scene between Gondibert and Editha, to which your Lordship objected, I have retained – but I have given it a turn, that I believe entirely removes the objection.

The concluding paragraph shows that Tiverton's friendly and generous former M.P. had given Hannah a copy of the famous Dictionary:

> Lest I should forget ... I take leave now to return my most humble thanks for the Johnson. I set so great a value on it, as a present from your Lordship that, when I heard the Robbers in the house, one of my first regrets was the Johnson, which I had no doubt that they would take away – and Mr Cowley as soon as he got down, to console me for my losses, sent to tell me that the Doctor was safe. I have the honour to be, with every thing that can be meant by respect and gratitude, Your Lordship's devoted and obedient servant,
>
> Hannah Cowley, Corporation Row.

Another shock was in store for Hannah. At Covent Garden, a new tragedy, 'Percy', by Hannah More, had been accepted. She was astonished and distressed to find that it bore strong resemblance to her own play;

> I can hardly describe my astonishment, or distress, when I saw Raby, the father of the heroine ... in a train of ideas exactly similar to those which I had given to the father of Albina, and that he even spoke several lines nearly verbatim, which will be found on comparing the two tragedies.[8]

Worse was to follow. Mr Harris put on another play by Miss More, 'Fatal Falsehood'. Hannah was greatly alarmed but thought it impossible that the 'same palpable resemblances could again happen'. They did. Cowley was dumbfounded to find that there were again blatant similarities. Cowley's character, Gondibert, is reproduced by More as Orlando, also a despairing lover who persuades himself that his beloved is receiving the addresses of another and gives himself up to the guidance of a scheming counsellor. Again, as Gondibert does, Orlando stabs the wrong person in the darkness and again the person supposed to have been murdered turns up at once to resolve the whole situation. Cowley's concern was to make it clear that the plagiarism could not be laid at her door; her tragedy 'Albina' had been written long before More's 'Percy' and 'Fatal Falsehood' appeared.

Clearly Cowley had been shabbily treated - her 'Albina' had been with Garrick when 'Percy' was being written and with Mr Harris when 'Fatal Falsehood' was under consideration; the most charitable view is Cowley's own 'I know that managers are continually giving advice', but an acrimonious correspondence between the two women did take place.

This overt quarrel signalled a 'first' in the history of 'Letters to the Editor': it is important because both letters throw a light on the social 'mores' and interdicts of the late eighteenth century. Printing the letters in full, *The Gentleman's Magazine* of August, 1779, declares 'The following Letters (from the *St James's Chronicle*) have been judged worthy to be preserved, as the Writers are both well known to the literati'.[9]

Hannah More, writing from Bristol, underlines her reluctance to appear in the public press, 'a step so repugnant to my own feeling, and to the delicacy of my sex' that she only took it to clear her name of plagiarism. 'I never saw, heard or read, a single line of Mrs Cowley's Tragedy'. She did not deign to 'enter into a newspaper altercation' and would not make any further reply.

Hannah Cowley replying three days later, 13 August, from Spa Fields, London, also stressed the 'indelicacy of a newspaper altercation between women, and of the ideas of ridicule which the world were apt to attach to such unsexual hardiness'. Hannah declares that she knew nothing of the 'frequent messages and menaces' which More had laid at her door; she had played no part in the accusations of plagiarism which had appeared in the St. James's Chronicle but adds (as well she might), 'I cannot say that I was sorry to see them or that I did not think myself obliged to the critic of that paper'. For her, too, the correspondence was now closed: her tragedy 'Albina' had gone to press and in the Preface both Miss More's 'Percy' and her 'Fatal Falsehood' were dealt with; she would not alter a single line of her Preface, 'I have only related events; let them speak for themselves'. Hannah's Preface details the whole sorry business.

Today, this may sound like a storm in a teacup but it was indeed the talk of the 'literati', and of the town for a long time. It could hardly be called 'a bad press' from Hannah's angle but the whole relationship between More and the Garricks must have been hurtful. Hannah had been generous in attributing to Garrick much of the success of 'The Runaway'. 'Unpatronized by any name, I presented myself to you, obscure and unknown. You perceived dawnings in my comedy, which you nourished and improved. With attention and sollicitude, you embellish'd and presented it to the world.'

By 1777, she was conscious that the relationship had deteriorated; when she last visited Garrick in the Spring, she felt that she was not altogether welcome and decided that a special pretext was needed if she were to call again. Knowing of his love of books, she had 'The Runaway' prepared in a special binding which she knew he particularly liked, wrote a personal dedication in it and asked her husband Thomas, to take it to the Adelphi where the Garricks were then living. However, the gesture failed because each time Thomas was denied entry by Garrick's servants 'in the most insulting manner'. Hannah then wrote to Garrick explaining what had happened and that the book had been meant as an 'apology for Mr Cowley's intrusion, or mine, whenever we might be admitted'. Garrick replied deploring his servants' attitude and asking the Cowleys to call the following Sunday morning.

The truth of the matter seems to be that wittingly, or more possibly unwittingly, Garrick did transmit to More the gist and many circumstances of Hannah's 'Albina'. He was in very poor health which may have made him careless in such matters. There is no doubt that he doted on young Hannah More who had come to London in 1774 with her sisters from Bristol, bearing introductions to London society through Sir Joshua Reynolds. She had ingratiated herself with Garrick and his wife by her fulsome praise of his acting, and even written an ode to his dog 'Dragon'! The great man was flattered. He nicknamed her 'Nine' after the Nine Muses and, childless as he was, treated her as his own daughter. She was a frequent visitor to his house in London and at Hampton. After his death, More not only eschewed the theatre and all its works but outrightly condemned playgoing as immoral. She refused to go and see Mrs Siddons in a revival of her controversial tragedy 'Percy', 'with which Garrick had given her a good deal of help'.[9] She left London and sought the company of the clergy and philanthropists, writing occasional tracts; on her death in 1833 she bequeathed her fortune to charities and religious institutions.

It says much for Hannah's determination and her belief in her own ability that she overcame what at the time must have seemed an unbearable snub from the man who had first recognised her talent, promoted her play and appeared a true friend. Courage was needed; in that, Hannah was never found wanting. Again and again Hannah shows in her plays that high courage is absolutely essential for the personal freedom of choice which she advocated; if Emily had not dared to run away ('The Runaway'), she would have been disposed of to the despised Baldwin; Elizabeth would perforce have found herself married to the utterly boring Gradus ('Who's The Dupe?') had she not contrived otherwise.

In the Preface to 'The Runaway', Hannah had declared, 'I perceive how much of this applause I owe to my sex'. Now, she had discovered that there was a down side to being a woman, a vulnerable woman at the mercy of the all-male dominated theatre managements of the time.

ALBINA: A Tragedy with a near-happy ending
July 1779: the Haymarket

'Albina' portrays the effects of carefully-implanted suspicion in the mind of a young aristocratic warrior, the Lord Edward, who has been charged by the King with the honour of leading a great army of 10,000 to the Holy War in Palestine. (There is frequently a time limit specified in Hannah's plays which gives added urgency to the action - here Lord Edward is to leave England within three days.) Before setting off, Edward desires above all to marry Albina, daughter of the Earl of Westmoreland, widowed a little over a year. He is desperately in love with her and she with him, although she has some doubts about the propriety of remarrying even though the official period of mourning has passed; this early emphasis on her scrupulous honour is borne out throughout the play.

However, the play could very well have been entitled 'Editha' who is the mainspring of the action. Born to rank and fortune, Editha deeply resents her dependence on Albina to whom she is companion and lady-in-waiting, and is furiously jealous of Edward's devotion to Albina since she herself had been hoping to marry Edward and through him regain the status she had lost. When she hears that Albina has agreed to overcome her scruples and marry Edward the next day, she cannot restrain herself - 'Albina triumphs - and Editha scorn'd'; she will have to remain henceforth at 'grov'ling distance' and observe her haughty rival's bliss. She even bursts out to Albina:

> *'I, who boast ancestry as great as yours*
> *Am now dependent on your charity'.*

She refuses to be appeased by Albina's assurance of her continuing love and friendship and goes to find Gondibert, the brother of Albina's late husband.

The tragedy could equally well have been called 'Gondibert' because he is psychologically the hero; he is in a truly horrendous situation, obsessively in love with Albina (he always has been) and insanely jealous of Edward who outshines him in battle and tournament and is now to have his belov'd Albina. Editha finds him a ready accomplice in her plot to plant suspicion in Edward's mind and so destroy his love for Albina.

> *'A little word, that touch'd it with suspicion,*
> *Would, with a serpent's tooth, its raptures cure -*
> *Suspicion, once awaken'd, never sleeps'.*

At the first attempt to infiltrate Edward's mind, Gondibert does not succeed; Edward refuses to hear of Albina's alleged unfaithfulness and draws his sword. But the seed has been implanted and when Editha supports Gondibert's allegations, Edward is unable to resist the temptation to test the story. Editha arranges to be in conversation with Edward where he can see the entrance to Albina's apartment and, as planned, Gondibert, in disguise, mounts the steps and enters the chamber. The damage is done.

The wedding day dawns and Westmoreland is overjoyed at the prospect of seeing his beloved daughter wed to the distinguished and well-loved Edward. When Edward comes and reveals Albina's lack of chastity to which he has been witness, Westmoreland accuses him of outrageous slander and challenges him to a duel. Edward refuses Westmoreland's challenge, saying it would be unfair to the older man, but when the matter is put to the King, it is decided that the combat shall go ahead. Luckily, an old and loyal retainer, Egbert, had overheard the plot between Editha and Gondibert and arrives at the last moment to prevent the duel. As Egbert reveals the plot against Albina's honour, Gondibert admits 'Twas me thou sawest in Albina's chamber' and challenges Edward, but the King refuses him the right to honourable combat and banishes him from the kingdom.

Gondibert, never particularly stable, is now clearly deeply disturbed emotionally and Editha plays upon his mood of desperation and confesses she made him her tool in the plot. When she leaves, Gondibert rants wildly; he has lost his country and his reputation. Banished and dishonoured, he must wreak vengeance on Edward. Gondibert's 'murder' soliloquy shows his mind is now quite unhinged; he sees his hand stained in blood, 'my brain's on fire', he sees a vision of Albina with another lover, a blooming youth, and runs off wildly shouting that he'll die and take Albina with him to the grave. There is a danger he may succeed. Albina, after the excitement of her wedding day, retires taking one of the two candles in her apartment with her. However, Editha still nursing her grievances and rejecting the kindness which Albina shows to her is also abroad bemoaning her fate, and wishes every ill upon Albina.

'Kindlier is Hatred in her honest garb
Than stinging Pity in her meek-ey'd mask'

Edward enters and in the dim light mistakes her for Albina; he is about to embrace her when Gondibert rushes in to carry out the murder which he has vowed he'll commit and plunges his dagger into Editha, also thinking she is Albina. Edward attacks him and in the struggle, Gondibert stabs himself. Edward, distraught at the supposed death of his beloved Albina is about to do the same when Albina herself, aroused by the noise, arrives and he throws his arms round her. In his death throes, Gondibert confesses his guilt and Edward gives thanks that Albina has been preserved. The upright Westmoreland rounds off the play in a closing speech reminiscent of some early American films with a moral summing-up

'O, mark th' effects of passions unrestrain'd'

V
HANNAH
AND THE COSWAYS

Throughout this very unhappy time, Hannah had the support of her husband, Thomas, who was himself no mean writer; she was a devoted mother to her three children, Frances, Thomas and Mary Elizabeth; in her prologue to 'The Runaway', she says her 'Comic Muse' was 'a little blue-eyed maid with cheeks where innocence and health's display'd' and a ...'romping boy Whose taste is trap-ball and a kite his joy'. She confessed that she never became an habitué of the Green Room and it was said even avoided the first nights of her own plays. She was, however, very far from being a *hausfrau*; besides her family connections, she had the *entrée* to the 'high society' of the day which enabled her to depict with such authenticity the more worldly characters in her comedies. In particular, she was on friendly terms with another Tivertonian, the celebrated portrait painter and miniaturist, Richard Cosway (1740 - 1821) and his brilliant and talented wife, Maria.

Richard is still remembered in Tiverton from the oil painting he donated to his native town. It hangs above the vestry door in the ancient church of St Peter (1073). He wrote to the clergy, gentry and inhabitants of the town in 1784:[10]

Gentlemen,
I have the honor to request you will accept, at my hands, the picture representing 'The Angel delivering St Peter from Prison' as a small token of the respect I have for you, and for the affection I shall ever retain for my native town; to the prosperity and splendour of which, it will always be my ambition, by every means in

my power, to contribute.
I am, Gentlemen, with the highest esteem,
    Your obedient and devoted Servant, RICHARD COSWAY

Richard was actually baptised at Oakford, probably on account of an outbreak of spotted fever in Tiverton at the time. In 1755, he won the first prize ever given by the Society of Arts; recognising the talent of the 15-year-old, several prominent residents including the tycoon, Oliver Peard, contributed towards sending him to study art in London. Their confidence and generosity was rewarded. Richard became the outstand-

The Angel delivering St Peter from prison.
A painting by Richard Cosway, hangs in St Peter's Church, Tiverton.

ing miniaturist of the eighteenth century (his work has recently been marked with prestigious exhibitions at the National Portrait Galleries in Edinburgh and London and in America).

Richard quickly dominated the great and glamorous world of London which, under the spell of the Prince of Wales (later the Prince Regent) was as addicted as he was to the arts, architecture, 'style' and 'living it up'. The Cosways' Sunday evening receptions and concerts were renowned; they had moved to historic Schomberg House between St James's Palace and the Prince's new Palace, Carlton House. 'Pall Mall was blocked on these occasions with carriages, sedan-chairs, linkboys and lackeys, and everyone who was well known in society found their way to Mrs Cosway's receptions. Horace Walpole was often in the rooms, as were the beautiful Duchess of Devonshire, the Hon. Mrs Anne Damer, the Countess of Aylesbury, the Marchioness Townshend, Lady Cecilia Johnstone, Lord Sandys, Earl Cowper, Lord Erskine, Mrs Cowley, and others too numerous to mention'. There are frequent references to these concerts in Horace Walpole's letters. Clearly, Hannah was on intimate terms with Maria; our 'well-known litterateur' wrote a teasing little letter of apology to her friend:[11]

My dear Mrs Cosway

This morning I was informed that you had been extremely ill. I am - how foolish to say 'I am very sorry!' - that phrase is in the mouth of all the children of indifference. I am myself very ill, or instead of my daughter you would have seen me. But how can you whom I saw last Tuesday at Somerset House so well - how can you have been a long time ill? Yes, I saw you, yourself. [The reference is to Maria's self-portrait at the Academy Exhibition, no. 248]. If you can draw everybody as justly as the fair Maria, you will be the first portrait painter in the kingdom...
... Pray let me know how you are - and tell me that some morning of the coming week I shall be a welcome visitant.

Your ever affectionate
H. Cowley   Powis Place, Sunday Evening

The Honourable Mrs Anne Damer.
Pencil drawing on paper Henry E. Huntington Library & Art Gallery.

The Cosway milieu was an invaluable source of rich comic material for Hannah. The Hon. Mrs Anne Damer, leading sculptress of her day, is clearly the inspiration for 'Lady Horatia' in whose studio much of the action of Hannah's last play, 'The Town Before You', (Covent Garden 1794) takes place. It is hilarious; the con-man Tippy, castigating Lady Horatia as a 'block chopper' tries to illustrate how unlifelike the statues are by grabbing hold of a model's foot - but it is the foot of a living model who screams and exposes him as the fraud he is. The rich uncle of Asgill who is in love with Lady Horatia also disapproves of women daring to indulge in sculpture. 'My nephew in love with a stone-cutter - he may as well live in a quarry'. Here, Hannah Cowley, without preaching is showing how unfair, ridiculous even, was the current attitude to women sculptors. Today, we can rejoice in many great sculptures by women in museums, country parks, towns and countries world-wide.

Another reflection of contemporary high society attitudes which Hannah cannot have failed to note at Schomberg House is to be found in the humorous treatment of 'country cousins' such as the Pendragons, brother Bobby and sister Sophie, in 'Which Is the Man?' (Covent Garden 1782). Up from Cornwall where the aristocratic rake Lord Sparkle was only too anxious to know them when they were canvassing for him, he despises and denigrates them once they arrive on his doorstep in London. They are unimpressed and give an interesting outsider view of London society and morals at the time.

However, Hannah was certainly not in favour of the very loose moral standards current among the *haut monde*. She also refers in several places to the lax standards in France. She certainly knew of her friend Maria Cosway's affair with Jefferson, as depicted in the Merchant Ivory film, 'Jefferson in Paris'. Jefferson (1743-1826) was older than Maria; he had succeeded Benjamin Franklin as the United States envoy to France and found it impossible to resist the charming, talented and vivacious Maria who at the time was semi-estranged from her peacock-vain husband strutting about in his extravagant and bizarre shoes and waistcoats.

Hannah's close friendship with the lovely and talented Maria even led to her meeting Jefferson. Maria asked Hannah who was going to Paris early in 1789 to take Jefferson a private letter as well as the usual letter of introduction which reads:

> Give me leave to present you Mrs Cowley the first dramatic author in this country, she has most distinguished talents, she is the most elegant writer, great poet, and a great genius, a particular friend of mine and an amiable woman. You have I hope some friendship for me, speak of me with Mrs Cowley, you will like her, take care of your heart, she may run away with it. How I envy her, and everybody that can converse with you. Pray write, pray write, and don't go to America without coming to England ... [12]

Again, later, she refers to Hannah in glowing terms:

> I hope you have seen her, how do you like her? Talk of me with her, she is sometimes too partial but she is a friend of mine, a woman of great genius and abilities and I love and estime her much ... [12]

Besides her family, and the Tiverton connection with the town's Member of Parliament, Lord Harrowby, who much admired her work, Hannah had not only friendship with the Cosway circle but even that of the Palace. Queen Charlotte had attended a Royal Command performance of 'The Runaway' and, in dedicating her next, and most successful play, 'The Belle's Stratagem' (Covent Garden 1780) to her, Hannah sealed a long friendship: in a dissolute age, Hannah and the Queen both deplored the immorality rife in London and on the continent at the time.

Hannah was, then, far from being one of the solemn 'blue-stocking' brigade. *The Gentleman's Magazine* of 1809 in the 'Biographical Character of the Late Mrs Cowley, states: 'In the different characters of daughter, Wife and mother, Mrs Cowley's conduct was indeed most exemplary. Her manners were lively and unassuming; her countenance was peculiarly animated and expressive!'

VI

THE BELLE'S STRATAGEM

The Brilliant Comedy

1780 Covent Garden

All the disappointment over management's handling of her tragedy, 'Albina' and all the unpleasantness over Hannah More's uncannily similar tragedies, completely disappeared when Hannah's next play, 'The Belle's Stratagem' was put on by Harris at Covent Garden in 1780. In 1707, a similarly named play by Farquhar 'The Beaux' Stratagem' had had some success. 'The Beaux' was a fast-moving romp describing the machinations of two young 'bloods' in search of love and fortune; it does not compare in characterisation and psychological insight with 'The Belle's'. Hannah's new comedy was hailed as a masterpiece. Again, though there is no stated protest, the message is clear; the unwisdom of pre-arranged marriages. Here Letitia Hardy, brought up in a wealthy county family, was promised by her father from childhood to Doricourt and the trouble arises when they meet as grown-ups. The 'contract' has been agreed and is now signed, sealed and settled, the 'consideration' being £80,000, contributed in equal shares, with the proviso that if either party reneges on the bargain, his or her share would be forfeited to the other.

Letitia is a beautiful young woman and all eagerness to meet Doricourt whom she has kept in her imagination since childhood; she is deeply in love with him. Doricourt, however, has just returned from the Grand Tour, he is very attractive and the darling of the smart set in town; he does not deny the beauty of his bride-to-be but finds her insipid and lacking that certain *je ne sais quoi* which makes the women of Italy and France 'resistless charmers'. Notwithstanding his disappointment, he is prepared to go ahead and honour the contract. He has reckoned without

Letitia. Although put out by his obvious indifference to her, she will not enter into a loveless union; she has a plan, she will heighten his indifference into positive dislike by posing as a gauche country lass, an embarrassing social misfit, so that he detests her; then, by contrast, when he discovers through the mechanism of a masquerade that the beautiful masked girl he has fallen in love with is none other than his betrothed, all will be well.

Letitia embarks on her stratagem which she recognises as a 'rash design'; but she is prepared to risk winning his love or losing him for ever 'never to be his wife will afflict me less than to be his wife and not be belov'd'. She casts aside the bashfulness that had afflicted her at their first meeting and brashly questions him on his travels - did he visit the countries where the men and women are all horses? And confides in him, (after all he is her 'sweetheart') that she had had other suitors in the country - the curate came a-suitoring and called her 'Venis and Junah and Dinah' but she discouraged his 'flimflams' saying a 'better man than ever trod in your shoes, is coming oversea to marry me' (that is, Doricourt), though now she is beginning to have her doubts - Parson Dobbins was the sprightfuller man of the two. She is a good actress and her hamming of a totally unsophisticated 'country cousin' fools Doricourt. He is appalled at the thought of marrying such an ignoramus.

The character of Doricourt is brilliantly portrayed from the very beginning when a journalist, Crowquill, calls on the porter at Doricourt's house in search of a story. All London is a-buzz with the news of the return of the rich, handsome Doricourt, Crowquill tells the porter 'I am the Gentleman who writes the *Tête à têtes* in the Magazines' to which the cynical porter answers that then he must be the fellow 'that ties folks together that never meet anywhere else'.

Not to be put off, Crowquill will reward the porter if he'll tell him a few anecdotes about his master, 'such as what Marchioness he lost money to, in Paris - who is his favourite Lady in town - or the name of the girl he first made love to at College (shades of William Jefferson Clinton,

President of the United States and the *enquête* - 1993 - into his life as a student at Oxford!!) - or any incidents that happened to his Grandmother or Great Aunts'. Crowquill is the forerunner of today's paparazzi, or 'rat-pack'; devious, underhand and plain corrupt, but he highlights the social prestige of Doricourt.

Can Letitia's scheme possibly succeed? At a grand masquerade, Doricourt is enchanted by the beautiful masked lady, dancing superbly and is determined to find out who she is. His indifference to Letitia had by now 'advanced 32 degrees towards hatred' because 'the creature's almost an ideot'. Yes, the paradoxical scheme is succeeding. Completely captivated, Doricourt declares 'By Heavens! I never was charm'd till now. English beauty - French vivacity - wit - elegance'. Of course, the unknown beauty is none other than Letitia; she refuses to reveal her name but promises she will take off the mask the next day 'in an hour when you least expect me'.

There follow complications. The incorrigible Flutter, who is a mass of misinformation about everyone and everything, tells Doricourt that the masked beauty is a 'kept woman', the mistress of Lord George Jennet. Doricourt is distraught and when Hardy, Letitia's father, attempts to persuade him that Flutter is, as usual, wrong, and the 'mask' is Letitia, goes off, in disbelief.

To expedite the ceremony, Hardy and his friends decide to pretend Hardy is on his death bed and his dying wish is for the marriage to go ahead. Meanwhile, Doricourt, in desperation at the prospect of having to marry the loathed Letitia has feigned madness in the belief that Mr Hardy will release him from his undertaking; but his friends insist he cannot deceive a dying man and he agrees by the bedside to honour his commitment. On emerging from the bed chamber, he finds the masked beauty awaiting him. As promised last night, she has turned up when least expected; moreover, he learns from her that she is certainly not Lord George Jennet's mistress and all confirm that the informant, Flutter, has as usual got it wrong. Doricourt, overjoyed to hear this, is declaring his undying passion for the masked beauty, when, wiping flour from his face, Hardy emerges and angrily demands how Doricourt dare make such declarations of love to the mask when he has just married Letitia, and explains his illness was just a ploy to make him marry Letty.

Doricourt is disgusted. He has no intention of being tied for life to the despised Letitia; his friend, Villers, sympathises, declaring 'how shocking a thing it is for a man to be forced to marry one woman, whilst his heart is devoted to another'. Doricourt announces that he will quit England for good, telling Hardy, 'the possession of my heart was no object either with you or your daughter. My fortune and name was all you desired and these I leave ye'.

His last wish is to implore the masked beauty to unveil so that he may carry with him into exile the one image of his heart. When, in great trepidation, she does so, Doricourt is in raptures. It has all 'come good'. Letitia explains how she was forced into her brave stratagem by his obvious indifference to her. He confesses he was wrong to mistake her 'delicate timidity' for the mark of an 'uninform'd mind or inelegant manners'.

There is a brilliant sub-plot which merges successfully with the main plot in the masquerade scene. Sir George Touchwood and Lady Frances, are recently married and they are in London because she is to be presented at Court after which her husband intends to take her back to complete rusticity in the country; he does not want her corrupted by contact with high society and town life. Lady Frances, on the contrary, is thrilled by the London scene and insists on doing the town with Mrs Racket and Miss Ogle, even though this incurs Sir George's displeasure. Later, at the masquerade, she is in danger from a typical philanderer, Courtall, who lures her to his apartment but a friend of Touchwoods, Saville, had seen through Courtall's plan and prevailed on Kitty, a lady of the streets, to wear a costume identical to Lady Frances' so that the rake carries off not Frances but Kitty. Lady Frances has had a shock but would still maintain her right to have some say in the conduct of her life and not be bundled off to obscurity in the country and Saville assures Sir George, 'Lady Frances was born to be the ornament of the Court ... '

All ends happily and Hannah has in a witty and fast-moving play demonstrated that a woman is entitled to a say in her own destiny and should not be content to be fobbed off with an emotionally indifferent husband (Doricourt) nor should she accept that a husband (Sir George Touchwood) may shape his wife's life entirely as he sees fit.

The play was Hannah's most popular and lasting success. Her clever use of the relationship between reality and illusion, which was to continue to fascinate her, contributed to its success. Truth can wear many faces; Letitia, bewitching her betrothed as the masked beauty presents her real self as opposed to the nature Doricourt supposed her to have. It had taken an artificial means, a mask, to reveal her intrinsic worth. Could this have been achieved without the medium of the mask? (A century later, Pirandello was to return again and again to this aspect of human behaviour, characters wearing a different mask to convey different aspects of their personality to suit differing circumstances.) No doubt it was this variety in the part of Letitia which made it a favourite with a great actress like Ellen Terry; the role incorporates at least three different acting opportunities; the downcast daughter undervalued by her suitor, the uncouth country lass and the spirited and irresistible masked beauty are all aspects of the true Letitia. 'The Belle's Stratagem' continued to be played until the end of the nineteenth century in America as well as in England and every performance instilled into the minds of the thousands of playgoers the thought that the current law debarring women from any legal right of their own must surely be wrong; the results were there vividly illustrated on stage for all to see. The climate of opinion changed gradually, though it was not until the passing of the Married Women's Property Acts of 1870 and 1882 that definite progress was seen to have been made. There was a long way to go before votes for women were won and equal pay but in the early days of the long struggle, Hannah played a significant part. Besides demonstrating how wrong the system of arranged marriages was, she shows that women themselves must play a part in the ordering of their lives. Had Letitia not acted out her little stratagem she would have found herself married to Doricourt on sufferance, she preferred to risk losing him altogether. Had not Lady Frances insisted on her right to enjoy the social and cultural whirl of London, she would have been whisked back to the country to a humdrum and boring life. Courage was needed.

The play was as popular with actors and actresses as with the public. Doricourt provided a brilliant part for 'Gentleman' Lewis, for 20 years stage manager and leading comedian at Covent Garden; the role he originally created was then played by Charles Kemble and later in 1866 by Sir Henry Irving who was so impressed that he revived the play as late as June 1876. It was given a further notable revival in April 1881 when Arthur Wing Pinero appeared in the small part of Saville. Ellen Terry who played Lady Touchwood in 1863 later moved to the starring role of Letitia which was acclaimed as 'among the most exquisite of her impersonations'.

Hannah, a staunch supporter of 'the Royals', had dedicated the play to her Majesty, Queen Charlotte. She of course knew the Prince of Wales (later the Prince Regent) through his friendship with the Cosways but the senior 'Royals' were much nearer to her upright moral stance and this the Queen especially appreciated. Her father boasted 'Mrs Cowley has had the honor to entertain their Majesties oftener than any other living author and it is known that the Queen had mentioned her more than once with very High Encomiums'.

The triumphant play continued to have royal support: Claire Tomalin in 'Mrs. Jordan's Profession' cites a report from a local paper, it was the autumn of 1802.

> Their Majesties George III and Queen, accompanied by the Five Princesses ... honoured the Richmond Theatre, for the first time, with their presence, to see The Belle's Stratagem and The Miser ... The House was crowded with all the beauty and fashion of Richmond and its neighbourhood and had to boast of the most brilliant audience that ever graced the Theatre.

Mrs Jordan was playing the 'star role' of Letitia Hardy, the very character that Hannah had outlined to the Queen in her dedication.

To the Queen

Madam,

In the following Comedy, my purpose was to draw a Female Character which with the most lively sensibility, fine understanding and elegant accomplishments should unite that beautiful reserve and delicacy which, whilst they veil those charms, render them still more interesting. In delineating such a character, my heart naturally dedicated it to Your Majesty ...

Madam,

With the warmest wishes for the continuance of Your Majesty's felicity, I am, Your Majesty's Most devoted and dutiful servant.

VII
'THE FIRST LITERARY FEMALE IN EUROPE'

Despite the acclaim which had greeted 'The Runaway' at Drury Lane in 1776, the new manager, Sheridan, who had succeeded Garrick, had 'shelv'd' it and the long run which could have been expected, did not materialise.

In 1780, the Cowley family was in serious trouble - lack of money. Earlier, on 8 November 1779, Tiverton Town Clerk, Beavis Wood, had written to his 'paymaster', Tiverton's former M.P., Lord Harrowby: 'Mrs Cowley treats with contempt all the abuse lately heaped on her; she has only received £30 for her Tragedy but is preparing another comedy'.

He was referring to the financial disaster of 'Albina' and to the forthcoming production of 'The Belle's Stratagem'. Lord Harrowby replied on 2 March 1780:

> I was very happy to see Mrs Cowley's comedy (The Belle's Stratagem) advertized and to read a favourable account of it since in a Newspaper. I know not what may not be expected of her spirits and genius, since it seems to have forced her play upon the Covent Garden Theatre. Her Courtship of the Management was rather rough, but the event seems to prove that she knew her ground better than her more cautious friends who would probably have advised gentler measures.[13]

Beavis Wood would have told Philip Parkhouse, his close friend and a Tiverton town corporator, of this letter for later in 1780, on 11

December, Philip himself wrote a personal plea to Lord Harrowby. Hannah's position had been detailed in the Preface to Albina; all the delays and vexations caused by the 'coalition of Sheridan and Harris (Covent Garden)' and 'their repeated breaches of appointments and promises' meant that Hannah 'had been deprived of a reasonable prospect of several hundred pounds and ... spent years of fruitless anxiety and trouble'. Philip outlined the position of Hannah and her family:[13]

> her husband by your Address has fifty pounds a year in the Stamp Office and gets fifty pounds a year more by his writing in a newspaper and this is all ... I beg your Lordship not to consider me as a Corporator of Tiverton, but as the Father of a woman who has done so much honor to her sex and Country ...

He points out that 'It had been in every Age and Court, a custom to pension some Dramatic writer' and cites a case in point, Kelly, a very poor writer, who rated four hundred a year. He continues, 'If it cannot be in the line of a Pension, surely a better Place might be given to her Husband. He has talents to do Honor to any situation that a Minister could place him in. He has a strong mind, great political knowledge ... and a Pen elegant and forcible - such a man and the Husband of Mrs Cowley ought not to spend his life among Footmen and Grooms below Stairs at the Stamp Office'.

Philip's plea for Hannah's husband, Thomas Cowley, to be promoted from his humble position in the Stamp Office was heeded. Thomas got a commission (Captain) in the East India Company. Hannah was under no illusion as to what this would involve. In 'Who's The Dupe?' 1779, Capt. Granger who wants to marry Elizabeth, the daughter of the rich 'rag trade' merchant, Doiley, is asked by his friend, Sandford, whether his influential brother has been able to help him financially:

Sandford: 'Will he put you in a situation to... ?'

Granger: 'Yes, to take a sweating with the Gentoos (Anglo-Indians - from Gentiles/Hindoos). He'll speak to Sir Jacob Jaghire to get me a commission in the East Indies'.

He goes on to mimic the very words his brother had used:

> *'you know, everybody grows rich there - and then you're a*
> *soldier, you can fight'.*

Granger: *(who has returned penniless from the war with America)*
'Yes, Sir Bob, I can fight; but I can't grow rich upon the
smell of gunpowder. Your true East India soldier is of a
different genus from whose who strew'd Minden with
Frenchmen, and must have as great a fecundity of
character as a Dutch Burgomaster. Whilst his Sword is
in his hand, his Pen must be in his cockade; he must be
as expert at Fractions, as at Assaults; today mowing
down ranks of soft beings, just risen from their
embroidery; tomorrow, selling pepper and Beetle-nut -
this hour a son of Mars, striding over heaps of slain; the
next, an Auctioneer, knocking down chintz and callico
to the best bidder'. (Act 1, scene 1).

Yes, 'employees' of the East India Company functioned in a dual capacity - as soldiers and as trade representatives (this equivocal situation had contributed to the downfall of Warren Hastings). However, from Thomas Cowley's point of view, this appointment considerably eased the family's budget problems; sadly, when it came, a posting to India for Thomas meant a very long separation from Hannah (the sea voyage took six months and Thomas was to die out there in 1797). However, although Hannah's eldest daughter, Mary Elizabeth, died at Tiverton whilst preparing to make the voyage to India to visit her father in 1789, the second daughter, Frances, not only visited her father in India but was married very happily on 19 July 1796 to an Oxford-educated clergyman, the Rev. David Brown, Senior Military Chaplain and Provost of the College of Fort William, Calcutta. He is referred to as founder of the Church Missionary Society.

It was, however, his daughter's peace and happiness that most concerned Hannah's father ... 'as her genius may one day fail her it will be poor satisfaction to have only the praises of a million or two of people' ... He points out, 'That Mrs Cowley is the first literary female in Europe cannot be disputed'.[14] He had good grounds for this claim; as well as the audience reached by productions in London and the provinces, the printed editions of her plays were read by a very wide public in America and on the continent. 'The Runaway' quickly reached four editions; it was published (probably as a piracy) in Dublin in 1776 and translated into German as 'Der schoene Fleuchtling' and published in Altenburg the same year and in Vienna in 1777. 'Who's The Dupe?' was published in April 1779 and 'Albina' first published in August 1779 was quickly followed by three further editions.

Philip Parkhouse's letter of 11 December 1780 was answered on 23 December; Tiverton's former M.P. promised to do his best for Hannah; apparently it was 'something substantial'.

Lord Harrowby's pulling of strings to obtain advancement for Thomas Cowley could well have been influenced by his own disappointment at the reception of 'Albina'; on his informal visits to his constituency he would have met the clever and attractive Hannah during his social chats with the Parkhouse family's friend, his own local 'minder', Beavis Wood. They would have enjoyed many a laugh about the Mayor's goings-on with his housekeeper, Miss Sally, about the Humorous Categorical Society which poked fun at local personalities and events, about Martin Dunsford, the leading local radical seeking reforms of the right to vote which might well have deprived Lord Harrowby of his seat. Hannah dedicated 'Albina' to Lord Harrowby:

TO THE RIGHT HONOURABLE
LORD HARROWBY

MY LORD
ALBINA had the honour of being known to your Lordship, almost from her infancy. Her faults, and her graces, You are already acquainted with, as she grew up in some measure beneath your Lordship's eye. She is now arrived at maturity; and if in her

present state, my Lord, you should find her more polished than when she had last the honour of your attention, it is chiefly owing to the hints with which you then favoured me.

I have the honour to be, My Lord,

> Your Lordship's grateful
>
> And obedient humble Servant,
>
> H. COWLEY.

Cleverly, this dedication applies equally to 'Albina' and to Hannah herself. Of course, the help which Lord Harrowby was able to arrange for the Cowley family was patronage but that was clearly the duty of Members in the late eighteenth century. Moreover, Lord Harrowby was aware that Philip Parkhouse was a valued corporator whose vote could count crucially in the election of the two Members of Parliament but the late eighteenth century should not be judged by today's criteria; yesterday's patron is today's 'sponsor' in his many guises.

The arms of Nathaniel Ryder, created 1st Baron Harrowby in 1776.

VIII
'WHICH IS THE MAN?'
February 1782 Covent Garden
(Thou shalt not disobey thy Guardian!)

Career Woman. That would be the label for Hannah today. She was a devoted wife and mother but took her work as a playwright and poet very seriously; she did not dwell upon the recent setbacks but went resolutely on. Her next play again illustrates the dire results that absolute power could have; not only did guardians in the eighteenth century have complete control over the destiny of their charges, they would go to great lengths to make this clear. If the ward had the effrontery to make her own decision, she had transgressed and must be punished.

Julia Manners has transgressed. Without obtaining the consent of her guardian, Fitzherbert, she has married hurriedly from her convent school in France, Belville, who unfortunately was immediately summoned to Florence on a diplomatic mission and had only time to beg her not to reveal their marriage until his return. Consequently, when she comes back to London, her guardian, Fitzherbert, knows nothing of this marriage. He had arranged for her to stay with the lovely young widow, Lady Bell Bloomer. Lady Bell had herself been a victim of the 'system', married to a 'husband to whom her father, not her heart, united her'; consequently, now the period of mourning is over, and with youth, health, beauty and a fortune on her side, she is playing the lady-about-town for all she is worth.

Meanwhile, Fitzherbert has not been idle in the discharge of his duty as guardian; he has found a prospective husband for Julia; pick'd him out from all the 'blockheads and fools' and invited him 'to take a fine girl off my hands with twenty thousand pounds'. However, the 'prospect' had told him that he was already married in France, about eight months ago, by an English Clergyman. He enthuses about his bride, 'Her beauty is of the Greek kind, which pleases the mind more than the eye. Yet to the eye nothing can be more lovely'. He boasts that the charming creature's name is - Julia Manners! and explains that, since he had to leave her so urgently, she had to remain in France; he was going to meet her at Calais shortly and bring her home to England.

Julia Manners! His very own ward! Fitzherbert is outraged. He says nothing to Belville to reveal that Julia is already in London and vows 'Ungrateful girl! Julia must be punished ... I have not deserved this want of confidence and must correct it ... Pendragon is a fit instrument ... Oh these headstrong girls!'

Pendragon (Bobby) and his sister, Sophy, are true country bumpkins, up from Cornwall to see the glamorous Lord Sparkle who, they had understood, would be overjoyed to see them after the very close friendship they had had with him in Cornwall where they had been instrumental in his gaining the Parliamentary seat. They have taken all Lord Sparkle's promises of a commission in the armed forces, of joining in the social whirl of London at face value, not realising the depths of his insincerity. Well aware of Pendragon's gaucheness, social inadequacies and total unsuitability, Fitzherbert takes Pendragon along to Lady Bell's to arrange a marriage with Julia. She is appalled; she cannot reveal that she is already married because of her promise to her husband, yet she cannot tolerate the addresses of the presumptuous 'suitor'. There is only one way out; she must get away and hide. Not only is she threatened with the preposterous Pendragon but the dreaded loose-living Lord Sparkle has openly stated that he will have the lovely widow Bell as his bride and as it's now the fashion to have a mistress into the bargain, he intends to have Julia in that role. Her maid, Kitty, says she knows the very place where her mistress can take refuge.

Life goes on - Lord Sparkle in hot pursuit of Lady Bell, and Lady Bell enjoying to the full every facet of London life. She may not be as superficial as at first supposed because towards Lord Sparkle's friend, a young officer, Beauchamp, who has been sent to acquaint Lady Bell of Lord Sparkle's love for her, she shows how much she wants to hear 'the genuine language' of love.

Meanwhile, Julia finds that the place of refuge which Kitty had found for her is none other than Lord Sparkle's house! She has been betrayed by the worthless maid and is now in the power of Sparkle who does not hesitate to show he really does intend to keep her as his mistress. As she tries to escape, Sparkle grabs, but, fortunately, Beauchamp comes in and rescues her from his clutches. That it was indeed a lucky escape is reinforced by the entry of the Pendragons who have come to demand satisfaction from Sparkle who had seriously trifled with Sophy's affections by giving her to understand that he had marriage in mind. Brother Bobby challenges Sparkle to a duel but the unscrupulous rake dismisses the whole affair as the result of two bumpkins not understanding the commonplace conventions and language of fashionable life.

More trouble is in store for the hapless Julia; no sooner has her rescuer, Beauchamp, taken her for safety to his own lodgings than the town busybody, Clarinda, arrives and Julia must for honour's sake hide in the next room. When, shortly afterwards, Belville turns up, Clarinda succeeds in forcing open the door of the room where Julia is hiding. Naturally, with so much subterfuge, Belville thinks the very worst; he will heed no explanations; the faithless Julia is dismissed from his life.

The mischief-making Clarinda takes Julia back to Lady Bell's apartments and explains to Lady Bell that she had been discovered in incriminating circumstances at Mr Beauchamp's place. Lady Bell is horrified; she can hardly believe it; her horror forces Julia into confessing the truth - that she is legally married to Belville. She explains the chain of events that led to her being discovered with the altogether innocent Beauchamp; all the trouble stemmed from her promise to her husband not to announce the news of their marriage until his return from Florence. Belville! Not Beauchamp! Lady Bell is mightily relieved and touched by the love Julia has kept for Belville, who now learns the truth

Hannah Cowley.
A portrait by Richard Cosway R.A.

and knows his suspicion was groundless. Fitzherbert confesses that he had never intended to do anything other than teach her a lesson by inflicting Pendragon on her.

The action moves on apace. Lady Bell is giving a 'rout' the kind of lively 'at home' when all London congregated for wine, women, song and cards (as at Maria Cosway's renowned Sunday evenings with which Hannah Cowley was familiar). The Pendragons have been invited along; society appreciates their oddity in manner and speech and will exploit their entertainment value. Sparkle, still full of self-confidence, enters to claim Lady Bell's hand but is met with reproaches by the Pendragons and by Belville who, now that he knows the truth, objects to his philandering with Julia. Sparkle is utterly discomfited. All ends well. Julia is reunited with Belville; the Pendragons will not be packed off back to Cornwall as Sparkle planned but may stay and enjoy London; and Lady Bell will marry Beauchamp. In closing, she declares Beauchamp shall continue his career as a soldier. 'One of those whom Love and his Country detain to guard her dearest, last possessions'. Beauchamp echoes her dedication to freedom and independence for England. It was 1782 and the audience would have appreciated these declarations knowing of the recent defection of America and conscious that the Napoleonic wars were closing in upon them. Hannah Cowley has been accused of 'jingoism' and her love of country often obtrudes to close a play as a kind of valedictory blessing. Perfectly acceptable then.

IX
'A BOLD STROKE
FOR A HUSBAND'
1783 Theatre Royal, Covent Garden

Hannah's next play, 'A Bold Stroke' was set in Madrid, probably to avoid outright confrontation with exponents of an Englishman's right, then largely unchallenged, to exact total obedience from wards, daughters and wives. By setting the piece in a foreign capital, she would deflect criticism that she was forever attacking an old long-established English custom; after all, the story concerned the *moeurs* of a country supposedly very different from those of England.

The Prologue explains the title words, 'Bold Stroke'. Hannah explains that 'The extreme succeeds beyond the patient mean' - boldness and courage were key elements in her philosophy. (Letitia in 'The Belle's Stratagem' had earlier given an example when, rather than just hope that her suitor's indifference would develop into true passion, she took the extreme measure of feigning blatant uncouthness and total lack of savoir-faire so that when her true personality was later revealed, it would trigger the genuine emotion without which she had decided not to marry at all.)

The main plot evokes a rake, Carlos, who has deserted his wife, Victoria, and family in the country for a mistress in town, Laura; she is calculating and avaricious and 'In a state of intoxication she wheedled me, or rather cheated me, out of a settlement'. Worse, it transpires that the property in question really belonged to his wronged wife (in England at that time a wife had no right to her own property, it automatically became that of her husband when she married!). Luckily for him,

Victoria does not take this situation lying down and, dressed in breeches and impersonating a young beau, Florio, insinuates herself into Laura's household. She then arranges for recovery of the deed by getting a go-between to impersonate her rich uncle, Don Sancho, who pooh-poohs the deed saying that it is certainly fictitious; the estate described certainly does not belong to his niece, Victoria, since it belongs to him. Furious, Laura tears up the deed. Victoria's bold stroke has succeeded; she regains the affection of her faulty husband and has preserved the family's fortune.

However, the sub-plot certainly steals the show. Don Caesar, father of Olivia (Victoria's cousin) has run out of patience with his daughter who is so perverse that she frightens off any prospective husband; he'll give her just two more chances before deciding to marry on his own account - perhaps the prospect of a mother-in-law will make her more compliant.

Suitor number one, Garcia, is quickly given an insight into Olivia's views on marriage; the full treatment. She pours scorn on 'mean compliance'; she despises 'milky wives' and when Garcia wonders why Don Caesar has never curb'd her forthright opinions, storms at him, 'curb'd?, Sir, talk thus to your groom - curbs and bridles for a woman's tongue!' Garcia (recalling the Taming of the Shrew) suggests 'perhaps you may meet a Petruchio, gentle Catherine, yet!' to which she retorts, 'But no gentle Catherine will he find me, believe it - Catherine! Why she had not the spirit of a roasted chestnut - a few big words, an empty oath and a scanty dinner, made her as submissive as a spaniel. My fire will not be so soon extinguished - it shall resist big words, oaths and starving'. Olivia is surely a precursor of the hunger-striking suffragettes of the twentieth century.

The very lively scene ends, needless to say, with Don Garcia making his excuses. In the post-mortem with her father, Olivia explains her attitude to Garcia; his conversation is 'like a parenthesis'. Don Caesar demands of his daughter, 'Like a parenthesis?' and she explains, 'Yes, it might be all left out, and never missed'.

Don Caesar is determined to off-load his daughter and sends an intermediary, Gasper, to let her know that his own marriage is imminent; this could mean that her fate will be to be 'immur'd in a convent for life' (a common solution to many daughter problems at that time). Olivia is in no way cowed; 'Immur'd in a convent! Then I'll raise sedition in the sisterhood, depose the abbess, and turn the confessor's chair to a go-cart'. Moreover, she refuses to believe Gasper's story. 'Marry, without my consent! No, no, he'll never think of it'. (A neat reversal of roles!) Nonetheless, her father returns to the scene of battle, chiding Olivia for discouraging suitors and recommending a very different approach, namely small talk about the weather, the ball, a cold, the latest scandal; in fact, to 'talk pretty little small talk'.

Suitor number two, her last chance, proves to be Vincentio, a young man of rank who is also a great music-lover. Obedient to her father's wishes, Olivia naughtily embarks on a tide of small talk. 'Tis a very fine day, Sir'; 'I caught a sad cold the other evening'; 'Pray was you at the ball last night?'; 'They say Lucinda has run away with her footman' etc. Vincentio is completely nonplussed and they quickly agree small talk is rubbish and turn to more positive subjects. Vincentio says he spends winters in Madrid but 'My summers I drawl through at my castle ...' and when Olivia says she would do the opposite and bring summer to the castle in winter by hanging green branches, 'the labour of silk worms' on the leafless trees and scenting the bushes with perfumes from Italy, Vincentio is ecstatic. They are getting on famously; but Olivia is only stalling. They move on to the subject of Vincentio's orchestra and concerts, and true to form, she plays her trump card. She says she can't stand a large orchestra but prefers one sole instrument (and when he has mastered that one instrument, she'll give him her hand) and the chosen instrument is - a harp. Vincentio is ready to agree but then she reveals that she means - a Jew's harp, nothing else. This is too much for Vincentio who goes off ...

Soon we understand Olivia's aversion to these suitors - she is in love with Julio; meanwhile, Don Caesar is going to carry out his threat and give Olivia a mother-in-law which could mean his daughter being relegated to an attic, if not immured in a convent. The intended young bride, Marcella, is just 19 and her father, according to custom, is perfectly willing to marry her off to Don Caesar, a man in his sixties. It seems that Marcella is doomed. She declares implicit obedience to her father's decision, but after some discussion with Don Caesar, the two of them agree that the affair shall only be in play. Marcella decides to warn Olivia of the plot against her. This leaves the way open for Julio and Olivia to come together which they do after a complicated meeting as the Prado with both Olivia and her cousin, Victoria, veiled. So a second happy ending has been achieved by another bold stroke; had not Olivia used all her wits and determination to avoid marriage to Garcia and Vincentio (not to mention previous suitors), she would have been locked into a wretched marriage.

X
'MORE WAYS THAN ONE'

1784 Theatre Royal, Covent Garden
Doctors (Feelove) and Lawyers (Evergreen) were also
Exploiters of the 'Wardship' system

When her husband as a Captain in the East India Company was posted overseas, Hannah must have been heart-broken; theirs had been a marriage dictated by love and harmony of minds which Hannah so clearly commends in her plays. When her father was interceding with Tiverton's former M.P., Lord Harrowby, for some financial support for the Cowley family, he had stressed Thomas's writing ability, and knowledge of the world and of politics. No doubt Thomas had been able to help and advise Hannah and probably explain the reality of some institutions such as the East India Company itself where the officers had to be both traders and military men at the same time. She dedicated her next play, 'More Ways Than One', to her husband: it appears he had been with her while it was being written for she writes in the Dedication:

> *'In blithesome mood 'More Ways Than One' had birth,*
> *Offspring of brilliant morns and eves of mirth;*
> *The laughing muse in sprightliest vein was by*
> *And 'quips and cranks' lay lurking in her eye'.*

Now, addressing him in distant lands, she feels the separation as keenly as he must do:

> *'Bid him not think, because I gaily write,*
> *That heavy hours to him, to me are light:*

and explains,

'My heart so keenly feels, 'twere death to live,
Did not bright spirits its strong sense relieve.
Through these, capricious, desultory, gay,
As though I felt not, glides th'unconscious day;
Through this I droop, I sadden, and complain,
Dragging, with pensive steps, life's length'ning chain'.

'More Ways than One', besides being a variation on the theme of the tragic consequences of the current practice of wards being given in barter by their guardians to totally unsuitable husbands, is a highly amusing satire on medical practice of the time. Dr. Feelove, (the name alone indicates his chief concern), had agreed a price of £15,000 for his lovely young ward, Arabella, the taker being his elderly (aged 60) friend, Evergreen. Dr. Feelove, while deploring that Parliament does not take action against 'quacks', is nothing but a pompous, ignorant quack himself. He is treating a patient, Bellair, as a terminally ill young man; a totally false diagnosis because Bellair is simply feigning illness to gain access to Dr. Feelove's house and bask in the sympathy and gain the love of young Arabella. When, later, Evergreen discovers this he threatens to make Dr. Feelove the laughing-stock of the profession by disclosing the whole story; moreover, since Arabella has been left alone with the 'patient', her reputation is sullied; he asks for an extra £5,000 for taking her on, 'shop soiled' as it were.

The sub-plot is original. Evergreen, too, has a ward, Miss Archer, who has the vivacity and independence of spirit so dear to Hannah (as first shown by Emily and by the 'rebel', Bella, in 'The Runaway'). Unusually, Miss Archer is a writer (could it be Hannah Cowley, relating one of her own experiences?) who has been cruelly lampooned in the poetry pages of the newspaper; no less than fifteen of her 'friends' have seen to it that she knew about it! The malicious verses have been written by the notorious Sir Marvel Mushroom, a parvenu of no 'background' but who has a hankering for literary renown and social status. He sportingly allows Carlton, a friend of the 'invalid' Bellair, to pretend to be the author of the 'send-up' so that he can meet the rather enigmatic Miss Archer, who is something of a loner. (Here again, Miss Archer resembles Hannah herself; it was well-known that Hannah stayed aloof from the back-stage intrigues of the theatre and from involvement in petty social politics).

There is a complicated intrigue where the young ward, Arabella, feeling forced to flee the Feelove household, unknowingly finds herself under the 'protection' of the detested Evergreen, but, thanks to Miss Archer, is able to escape; Miss Archer, however, takes her to what she thinks is a safe lodging only to discover that in fact the supposed lampoonist, Carlton, lives there. That he is not the true author of the vicious attacks is explained and the end result is two happy couples, Arabella with Bellair and Miss Archer with Carlton; and two disappointed avaricious old men. Dr. Feelove does not get paid by the calculating old Evergreen and Evergreen does not get his young bride.

The minor characters are, as usual, particularly well-drawn. Miss Juvenile plays the part of a young writer determined at all costs to get into print; the 'upstart', Sir Marvel Mushroom, has a French valet Le Gout who feels his master's lack of savoir-faire is a sorry reflection on himself and advises him on the finer points of etiquette. Besides the amusing insight into the medical and literary world of the day, the main purport of the play which shows up the system of wardship for what it was, grossly and ludicrously unfair, must have had a lasting impact on contemporary audiences and on subsequent readers of the printed plays. The drawbacks to arranged marriages have been highlighted again today in the twentieth century with the arrival of immigrants from countries where these are part and parcel of a national or religious culture. It would not perhaps be so easy for a twentieth century Hannah Cowley to use these as a theme for a play without giving offence; but the message is as relevant today. Surely women should be masters (or should that be mistresses?!) of their own destiny.

XI

ANOTHER ANTI-COWLEY CAMPAIGN

A School for Greybeards (or The Mourning Bride)
1786 Theatre Royal, Drury Lane

'A School for Greybeards' is not among Hannah's best plays. It depends heavily on disguise, intrigue and mistaken identities, but at the end of the play, the two 'Greybeards', Don Caesar and Don Alexis have been taught a lesson; the folly of taking or scheming to take a very young bride when they are in their sixties.

'Greybeard', Don Gasper, has used a totally dishonest trick in his determination to marry the 'Mourning Bride', Antonia. She had just exchanged vows with her beloved Henry when he was forced to flee the country (Portugal) to escape a writ for his execution on the charge of having fought a duel. Unscrupulous old Don Gasper has shown Antonia an untrue account of Henry's death at sea while on a voyage to Mexico. However, in exile in Madrid, Henry has learnt the wicked old man is planning to marry Antonia and hurries back to rescue her, posing as Don Julio.

The other 'Greybeard', Don Alexis, is already married to a very young and attractive bride, Seraphina, but is concerned that she is admired by others. He also has a daughter, Viola. The first 'Greybeard', Don Gasper, has a son, Octavio, who is not keen on marriage but is sent by his father to woo Viola. However, he mistakes the lovely young wife, Seraphina, for Viola; luckily for Don Alexis, Seraphina has a deep sense of honour; despite temptation, she will not deceive her husband; moreover, Octavio values his bachelor freedom.

The marriage of Don Gasper and Antonia is, however, imminent and Henry (disguised as Don Julio) will not get his pardon since Don Gasper has applied for it, calculating that if Henry were to return to apply for it, he would be told he couldn't be given it since it had already gone! So, Henry, too, is forced into subterfuge. He obtains from Don Alexis a 'seal-ring' which he takes to Don Gasper; both old men are counsellors of the realm and the seal-ring is an earnest of the urgent message that Henry brings; Don Gasper must go at once to Don Alexis to counter an immediate serious threat to the security of the nation. While he is out of the way, Henry has his chance; before the scheming old Don Gasper can return from his fool's errand, Henry comes on waving the pardon which he has obtained by personal approach to the Queen, and marries his beloved Antonia. Despite the many complications, this is a fast-moving play with sharp dialogue and some excellent delineation of character, particularly of Seraphina whose devotion to the 'marriage ethos' is very much in Hannah's idiom.

Jealousies and feuds between playwrights, producers and managements were as commonplace two centuries ago as they are today and Hannah certainly fell victim to a well-organised 'anti-Cowley' campaign in 1786. In the Address to the printed edition of 'A School for Greybeards', she describes what happened. At the first performance, there were persons present 'who went determined to disapprove at all events'; this was confirmed by reports in the press. Objection was taken on two counts; the indecency of some of the language and the affront to propriety of snatching away a bride already promised to the bridegroom.

Hannah vindicates herself on the first count by saying that obviously characters should speak in the fashion natural to them and quotes a celebrated critic as saying, 'When Mrs Cowley gets possession of the spirit and turn of a character, she speaks the language of that character better than any of her dramatic contemporaries'; this has been the opinion of subsequent critics in the last two hundred years. It is almost impossible to judge, after two centuries, whether the charge of lewd language was well-founded but to refute it Hannah had the play printed exactly as performed so that the public at large might decide for themselves. To an ordinary reader today, absolutely nothing exceptionable can be found and where there is one indication (Hannah marks it with an asterisk) of the matter complained of, it appears today to lack any improper connotation. Don Alexis (threatening his daughter Viola who has been found guilty of escaping from his house over the garden wall) says: 'bread and water, and a dark chamber, shall be your lot ...'. To this, Sebastian, with whom she has eloped and married unbeknown to her father, replies: 'No, Sir - I am the arbiter of her lot; however, I confirm half your punishment; and a dark chamber she shall certainly have'. What could the words 'a dark chamber' have meant to the eighteenth century audience? Hannah's footnote explains, 'This is the expression, I am told, which had nearly prov'd fatal to the Comedy. I should not have printed it, but from the resolution I have religiously kept, of restoring everything that was objected to'. Perhaps we shall never know: students from abroad have asked me to explain expressions from TV shows which they couldn't understand and yet people burst out laughing on hearing them: the list included 'he didn't come up to my expectations', 'she's got a bun in the oven', and 'she's got a lovely pair of Bristols'! Perhaps, writing as she so brilliantly did, in character (witness the Pendragons up from Cornwall so cleverly portrayed in their native Cornish mode of expression - and of morals; Le Gout, the French valet in 'More Ways Than One'; Gradus, the scholar from Brazen-Nose in 'Who's The Dupe?' and many, many others) Hannah did, wittingly or unwittingly overstep the mark; but that was part of her genius; mundane, witty or tragic, she lets her characters speak in their own idiom,. However, it is hard to suppose that there was any grave breach of good taste - vulgarity was not part of Hannah's make-up.

The second accusation, the impropriety of snatching Antonia from 'Greybeard' Don Gasper within minutes of the marriage ceremony is even harder to uphold. Don Gasper has tricked Antonia into thinking her true betrothed, Henry, is drowned and furthermore ensured that Henry can never get a pardon for his crime of duelling by arranging to buy it himself. What could be more dishonest? How this rescuing of Antonia from such a man could cause offence is all the more difficult to appreciate since Hannah states in her introductory Address that the idea of the Don Gasper, Antonia, Henry situation had come to her from an obsolete comedy, Aphra Behn's 'The Lucky Chance (1687) set in the city of London. Hannah had, however, transferred the action to Portugal using 'nobler' characters. The snatching of the bride had not then aroused any objection, so why was it condemned as 'ill-conceived' a hundred years later? Part of the objection might have been due to the incipient prudery of the late eighteenth century but, more probably, there were other forces at work: jealousy of Hannah as a playwright and a woman playwright at that and also envy of her reputation as a poet.

Although it is as a playwright that Hannah Cowley is valued today, she was very much in the limelight as a poet in her lifetime. Under the pseudonym of Anna Matilda, she carried on a poetic and sentimental correspondence in *The World* with Robert Merry or 'Dells Crusca', the name he took from the literary academy founded in 1582 to 'purify' the Italian language. This had attracted the notice of the *'literati'* and even that of the venomous critic, Robert Gifford, who denigrated it in the *Baviad*.

Her first long poem, 'The Maid of Arragon', was published in 1780; it is a tale of filial piety fittingly dedicated to her father, Philip Parkhouse. He had early recognised Hannah's talent and encouraged her; this she acknowledged:

> *Yours then the meed, if meed kind Fame will grant,*
> *The tale to you, to you the bays belong;*
> *You gave my fancy wings to soar;*
> *From your indulgence flows my wild note song.*

More important was Hannah's second longish poem, 'The Scottish Village' (1786) which can fairly be claimed to show Hannah as one of the very first of the 'environmentalists'. The trigger was the news that lovely Pitcairne Green in Scotland had been marked down as the site for an extensive village, or in modern parlance 'new town'. She confesses in the Preface to having dropped a tear when she read of the grand ceremonies to launch it and considered what such an invasion might mean in her beloved Devon. What might become of the high hedges of hawthorn, sweetbriar, myrtle and a thousand flowers and of the sloping woods, 'painted meads' and 'fields of burnished corn waving like a golden sea' now and then glimpsed beyond?

Moving on to the 'hour of change', she deplores that

> *The verdant face of this once happy plain*
> *The sharp-tooth'd mattock shall deform, tear ...*
> *The future Town, submissive to their will*
> *Rises from Earth and spreads its skirts around.*

However with her characteristic sense of fairness, she then dwells on the advantages that might follow, once Scotland's 'grand staple' is established. Once the looms are at work, she foresees a happy outcome. There may

> *the rich damask spread its fruit and flowers*
> *for royal tables, and for halls of state:*
> *There the transparent lawn display its powers,*
> *To soften beauty, and new charms create.*
> *Go, Manchester, and weep thy slighted loom –*
> *Its arts are cherish'd now in Pitcairne Green!*

She pictures the harbours thronged with ships and, happily, industrial success might well lead on to seats of learning which would nurture scholars, poets, lawgivers, philosophers.

As ever, Hannah Cowley includes women in the rosy future:

> *Yes, whilst the laurel crowns the manly head*
> *The blossoms for the fair shall gladlier blow*

and goes on to pay tribute to two outstanding contemporary women poets, Anna Letitia Barbauld and Fanny Burney.

> *Yes, such as these, thy plain may one day boast.*

She ends by confessing that her early 'falling tears' have given way to optimism. Hannah was profoundly religious and concludes:

> *Yes! the great Guardian of the general weal*
> *Ne'er gives a Mis'ry but he sends a cure.*

Hannah was well aware of the jealousy which besets the writer and the poet. Garrick, Sheridan, Hannah More, far from welcoming her to their ranks after the success of 'The Runaway' had been, at best obstructive, at worst downright hostile. In 'More Ways Than One' (1784) she had depicted the literary scene of the epoch; Miss Archer, a successful poet and something of a loner (not unlike Hannah herself) has been unfairly lampooned in the papers by the publicity-seeking ignoramus, Sir Marvel Mushroom. Typical of the literary rat-race, friends flock round to tell her the news of her public discomfiture. How far the success of 'The Scottish Village' contributed to the animosity shown towards Hannah and the 'Greybeards' is difficult to assess. It was a totally new subject for discussion; the rights and wrongs of taking greenfield sites for development was not then the contentious issue it has become 200 years later. But the very novelty would have exposed Hannah to criticism from many sources, not least rival playwrights and poets.

The hostile reception of her 'Greybeards' was very hurtful to Hannah. With no supportive husband to reassure and encourage her (Thomas has sailed for India in 1783), she confesses that all the criticism had had a dampening effect on her spirits. 'I feel encompassed with chains when I write, which check me in my happiest flights, and force me continually to reflect, not, whether this is just? (i.e. appropriate), but, whether this is safe?' (The address to 'A School for Greybeards).

There could be several explanations of the campaign mounted against Hannah. Sheridan was none too pleased to have a rival name on the theatre boards: he also may not have approved of Hannah's devotion to the Royal Family. Patriotism figures very largely in several of her plays; as the wife of a serving officer, she would feel even greater loyalty and have more appreciation than most people of the perils facing England not only from France but further afield. Sheridan and Fox were more intent on wooing the Prince Regent and decrying the King and would not have been averse to making fun of hand-on-heart attitudes to the establishment. Moreover, Hannah advocated morals, especially in marriage, very far from coinciding with their much more elastic views.

The play was apparently 'roughly received' on its first night at which Hannah was not present. This is borne out by the reliable historian, John Genest, in *Some Account of the English Stage from the Restoration 1660 - 1830*, p. 427, 'the audience took needless offence at a scene in the Fourth Act and an unfortunate expression in Young Bannister's part'. Bannister was acting Don Sebastian in love with Viola. Genest continues, 'It is a good Comedy and very well acted' and whilst rebuking Hannah for not more fulsomely acknowledging Mrs Behn's play 'Lucky Chance' which Hannah had admitted gave her the idea for 'Greybeards', says of Aphra Behn's play that 'it is too indecent to be ever represented again'. Maybe the audience was visiting the sins of Behn upon Hannah! In any case although Hannah claimed 'many brilliant and crowded nights', it was not one of her successes, neither stagewise nor moneywise.

XII
'THE FATE OF SPARTA
(or The Rival Kings)'
1 January 1788 Drury Lane

In any assessment of Hannah's contribution to the 'cause' of femi-
nism, it is important not to underestimate the impact that this
tragedy would have had. It would have attracted more intellectual
audiences than those which flocked to her first uproarious comedies and
also many subsequent serious-minded readers of the published edition.
In the comedies Hannah had well and amusingly demonstrated the
bizarre result of women being totally subservient to men, whether
guardians or husbands. In 'The Fate of Sparta' we see a women in a
nobler, heroic role; despite conflicting loyalties, split between father and
husband, Sarah Siddons playing Chelonice shows a woman who, determined to do what she personally sees as right, becomes the 'first woman
Ambassador for Peace' in a war-torn world.

The Dedications and Prefaces to her plays give an insight into Hannah's
personality and the vicissitudes of her life which are the chief source of
our knowledge of her (apart, of course, from the plays themselves). 'The
Fate of Sparta' she dedicated to John Cowley Esq., brother to her
husband, Thomas, as a mark of personal respect. 'It is delightful to make
an offering to those we love' and she expresses the hope that his children
and her own may enjoy the same mutual friendship. John Cowley was a
City merchant dealing largely in corn but he was also something of a
scholar because Hannah comments that he is likely to notice deviations
in her tragedy from the story as told by Plutarch in his 'Life of Agis' on
which her play is based, though she adds that, although she may have
altered events, she has strictly abided by character.

Hannah says she had been drawn to this tale of Sparta by her admiration for Plutarch's subtle yet powerful delineation of the character of the heroine, Chelonice. 'I wondered such a character had never been brought on the Stage, to do honour to her sex; yet I had joy in reflecting that this was precisely the age in which it ought to be done, for this age boasted a Mrs Siddons'. Chelonice, torn between the love of her father, Leonidas, and of her husband, Cleombrotus, offers tremendous dramatic opportunities and proved a perfect vehicle for the undoubted talents of Mrs Siddons in conveying pathos and despair.

The alternative title of 'The Rival Kings' is perhaps the more appropriate. One of the two kings, Cleombrotus, husband of Chelonice, has been deposed by Chelonice's tyrannical father, Leonidas, who is in command of the city of Sparta. Cleombrotus, with an army of mercenaries, is encamped outside the walls bent on retaking the city and regaining his crown. Torn between love of her husband and of her father, Chelonice has thought it her duty to go to Leonidas' side. Determined to prevent the attack which, besides leaving her either without husband or without father, would be disastrous for Sparta, she steals out from the city at night, disguised as a priestess, to plead with her husband in the hope of averting the attack. She counsels peace but, forced to unveil, only achieves a stay of execution for one night. On hearing of her escapade when she returns, her father far from acceding to her pleas to make peace with Cleombrotus, orders her to entice him to the grove where he can be murdered. She refuses and she and her infant son are put in chains.

Meanwhile, the villain of the piece, the ambitious Amphares who covets both the throne and the hand of Chelonice agrees to do what she had refused to do - lure Cleombrotus to the place where he can be conveniently killed, but in the darkness, instead of killing Cleombrotus, he runs a dagger through his own good brother, Nicrates. When, therefore, Cleombrotus comes on the scene, Nicrates, just before dying, is able to warn him that Amphares, far from being the friend that Cleombrotus supposes him to be, covets his throne and his wife and that Chelonice has been cast into chains.

The mercenaries, in defiance of Cleombrotus' order decreeing a one night's respite, have begun to attack the city walls. Leonidas has had his daughter released and she is momentarily reunited with her husband who, as a matter of honour, goes to drive back his disobedient troops. He succeeds but, surrounded by Amphares and his forces, has to take sanctuary in the Temple where the vengeful Leonidas would have had him put to death but the soldiers refuse to do the deed within the sacred Temple walls. Chelonice pleads with her father to spare Cleombrotus' life but Leonidas says he will only do so if he is banished for ever and wants Chelonice to consent to stay in Sparta and become Queen of Sparta at his side. She, another example of Hannah's exemplary and loyal wives, chooses to go with her husband and child into exile.

Poetic justice is done. Before the deposed Cleombrotus, his wife and child leave for their exile, Amphares who has not renounced his ambitions to rule Sparta, murders Leonidas. Hearing the groans of his dying father-in-law, Cleombrotus fights and defeats the traitor and, before expiring, Leonidas is able to give his beloved daughter and Cleombrotus his blessing.

It is important to see this play in the context of the time; tragedy was considered a nobler genre than comedy and audiences, used to sitting through Sunday sermons measured by a strict hour-glass, would not have become restless. The many changes of scene would also have helped sustain interest in what could have been a static play; the action moves from the Camp beneath the Walls of Sparta to the Palace of Leonidas, the Tent of Cleombrotus, the Tribunal, the Prison, the Grove, a Colonnade at the Palace and the Temple of Minerva. It is unlikely, however, that as Hannah had wished in her Dedication, her own children and those of her brother-in-law, John Cowley, will 'wander again and again over this page, after the hand which traces it moves no more'. It is difficult today to understand Chelonice's utter devotion to her tyrannical father, though of course filial duty was very much more to the forefront in the eighteenth century when fathers were there to be obeyed and their will done in all things. This, almost obstinate, devotion of Chelonice would have been an interesting talking point in the salons of the day. Again, Hannah had done a service to the 'cause' of women, drawing attention to the dilemma this time not of a man (Hamlet, Othello, Macbeth etc., etc.) but of a woman, so often faced then as now with choices entailing grave emotional and sometimes tragic results.

XIII
ANOTHER SPITEFUL ATTACK

'A Day in Turkey (or The Russian Slaves)'
1791 Covent Garden

This was a triumph; it had its premiere on 3 December 1791 and was a true 'spectacular'. The brilliant scenes are constantly changing, a Turkish Camp in the Forest, the Garden of the Bassa (Turkish Overlord) with palms, fountains and decorations in the Eastern style, the high-walled Garden behind which the ladies of the harem lived, a Prison, the magnificent Apartments of the Bassa. There are dances, marches, songs: of one, sung without instruments, a footnote to the first edition reports 'these lines ... are always followed by rapturous applause'. Professor Link describes it, aptly, as a comic opera and Hannah would have known all about the making of a successful piece like 'The Beggar's Opera' by John Gay. Up at Barnstaple, her father's mother was Gay's first cousin, close friend and confidante. She took great pains to give detailed instructions even on the small matter of the 'sofa' (throne) which must have a canopy 'composed of two umbrellas of white satin, each trimmed with gold fringe, festoons of flowers and tassels'. The music for the songs and dances was specially composed by Mazzinghi.

The comic element is centred on the character of A La Greque, valet to Count Orloff, a Russian nobleman taken prisoner by the Turks. When he realises that both he and his master, the Count, now have the same status of slave, the cheeky rogue immediately claims absolute equality with the Count; indeed, he flaunts his superiority since he can sing courtly airs, use the powder puff and coif hair, whereas Orloff is only good for fighting. He reassures his master, 'I'll treat you with great condescension, depend on't and endeavour to make you forget the distance between us'. When he is taken before the Bassa Ibrahim, A La Greque stresses that he is no Russian like his master but French and that he only went to Russia 'to polish the brutes a little and give them some ideas of the general equality of man ... but they still believe that a prince is more than a porter'. The rascal is even able to find a way to climb the harem wall and talk to the ladies. At the end, when Count Orloff and the Bassa Ibrahim have declared their friendship and respect for each other, he is not at all dashed by the turn of events. Knowing that he will lose dignity on returning to his former role of 'duteous servant', he impudently tries to wangle a job with the Bassa as his head slave-master. A La Greque is very well drawn and, at the time of the French Revolution, would be a more political animal than an English valet, so his allusions to liberty, equality, fraternity would be very much in character but these were the basis of yet another spiteful attack on the playwright.

Hannah was accused this time of dabbling in 'politics'. In her Preface to the first edition (17 February 1792) she says, 'Hints have been industriously circulated that the following comedy is tainted with politics. I protest I know nothing about politics; will Miss Wollstonecraft forgive me - whose book contains such a body of mind as I hardly ever met with - if I say that politics are unfeminine?' Hannah was never a hard-line feminist although she could not have been unaware of the political scene of the day. However, she had fallen foul of those who were bent on reading into the utterances of A La Greque a significance which could hardly have been there; as she says 'How could I bring an emigrant Frenchman before the public and not make him hint at the events which had just passed, or were then passing, in his native country? ... It is A La Greque who speaks, not I'. She found it difficult to forgive these critics because their unfair aspersions deprived her play of the honour of a Royal Command Performance. On the second night, the passages complained of were omitted but then immediately restored and the first edition contains the original script.

The story-line is believable and original. Alexina, a beautiful young Russian bride has been kidnapped by Turks on the very day of her wedding to Count Orloff who then joins the Russian army to facilitate his search for her in Turkey. However, he himself gets captured and has the status, as does his valet, of a slave. The Bassa Ibrahim naturally wants to have his new slave, Alexina, brought to him (another concubine for the harem would be her fate) but, luckily, on a visit to the harem garden, he mistakes another Russian prisoner, the peasant Paulina, for his intended mistress and falls in love with her. All, therefore, can end happily because when, finally, Orloff finds his wife, he discovers that it was Paulina, not Alexina, that he saw in the arms of Ibrahim.

Paulina, her brother and father are Christian Russians who have been captured by the Turks and is fortunate in that a kindly harem overseer, Mustapha, has bought her as a companion for Alexina. She tells him that she would very much like to see her father and brother again and Mustapha promises, 'Well, if you behave discreetly, I'll buy your father and brother Peter'. At this, Paulina bursts out, 'Buy! Buy! Why, you talk of buying us, as though we were baskets of eggs or bales of cotton'. Mustapha replies simply, 'Yes, it is the mode here' but adds wittily, 'we are so fond of liberty that we always buy it up as a rarity'. As for the ladies of the harem, they simply can't see why Bassa Ibrahim is attracted to the Russian slave (Paulina); Fatima, one of the ladies of the court, confides to a friend, 'What an odd whim it is in our master to grow fond of the mind of a woman. Did ever anybody hear of a woman's mind before as an object of passion?' To which he replies, ' I don't understand it'.

There are other references to the status of women. An Italian slave, Lauretta, is told by the extremely unpleasant harem-master, Azim, that he is looking for the new French slave, A La Greque, because there is no way of guarding against Frenchmen for 'they make free everywhere'. To which Lauretta replies, 'At least they have made themselves free AT HOME! And who knows but at last the spirit they have raised may reach even to a Turkish harem and the rights of women be declared, as well as those of men'. There speaks the authentic voice of Hannah Cowley as a herald of the emancipation of women; marriage should never be debased to the level of a business transaction, love should include the mind as well as the body, and women, too, have rights as well as men. Could this be the 'politics' to which the detractors of the play itself and of Hannah herself were referring?

XIV
HANNAH'S LAST PLAY
'THE TOWN BEFORE YOU'
1794 Covent Garden

Sadly, 'The Town Before You' was Hannah's last play: she dedicated
it to Mrs Frushard of Calcutta who was, apparently, a much-
respected hostess and friend in her 'elegant pavilions at Gassary',
helping everyone in an unassuming way. She must have been a great
comfort to Thomas Cowley in his lonely exile with 'John Company' and
to Hannah's second daughter, Frances, who had gone to join her father,
after the death of her sister, Mary Elizabeth, who had been preparing to
make the six months' voyage out to India. Hannah must, indeed, have
felt lonely and she had, too, to meet unsupported all the spiteful and
undeserved criticisms levelled against her and her plays.

With the theatre, too, she was disillusioned. In the Prologue, she
laments the decline of true theatre which had given way, by public
demand, to slapstick, where honest sentiment and humour is replaced by
stage 'business' with clumsy sword play and people falling off chairs, all
in aid of the pursuit of the desire to 'Laugh, laugh, laugh'. Hannah
laments, 'Let Sadler's Wells and the Circus empty themselves of their
performers to furnish our stage; the expense to Managers will be less and
their business will be carried on better. The understanding, discernment
and education which distinguish our modern actors, are useless to them;
strong muscles are in greater repute, and a grimace has more powerful
attraction'.

Despite her strictures, Hannah's last play is one of her most lively and
gives a fascinating picture of the London of her day. It opens with a very
sharp quarrel between Oxford-educated Fancourt and his second wife; he

is talking high-falutin' nonsense about poverty being altogether nobler than riches and backing his argument with a translation from the Greek; clearly his much-abused wife does not agree with him. He complains about a squalling child and she retorts that the children cry because they're hungry and he won't bestir himself to earn a living; they are, moreover, the children of his first marriage; Fancourt sneers that he only married her anyway because she had some money; he is, in modern terms, a cad and a rotter. By a stroke of luck, he then proves his point that idleness can pay off when 20 guineas arrive from an admirer of his, Sir Robert Floyer, recently High Sheriff of Glamorganshire, now knighted, who has just come to London with his lovely and spirited daughter, Georgina, to seek the high office and status that he thinks he deserves.

Far from being genuinely grateful to his benefactor, Fancourt quickly shows himself as a crook when he conspires with con-man, Tippy, to 'do' the Welsh knight. Tippy who lives entirely by his wits has been cashing in on his resemblance to a Lord Beechgrove which is so uncanny that he had gate-crashed private parties, stayed in the best hotels, all by exploiting the fact that he is the Beechgrove double. Fancourt introduces his fellow-crook to Sir Robert as Lord Beechgrove and is able to persuade the social climber that some great office of state could easily come his way by cultivating his lordship, mentioning that Beechgrove (i.e. Tippy) would, he knows, appreciate the loan of £1000 because he is a 'little out at present' and does not want to borrow from Jews. The swindle nearly fails, however, when Sir Robert complains to Fancourt that he's been snubbed one morning in the Park by Beechgrove so he certainly won't be lending £1000 to a man who cuts him dead. Fancourt realises his path must have crossed with the real Beechgrove and succeeds in persuading Sir Robert that Beechgrove must be forgiven such a temporary lapse because he is so important, 'a man whose head is stuffed with the business of all Europe'. Fancourt then tries to double-cross Tippy by not paying him his share of the £1000 but doesn't succeed.

Tippy's role is not finished. He is scheming with the help of Georgina's maid, Jenny, to induce the beautiful young heiress to visit the waxworks near his lodgings, and get her compromised; then 'marriage must follow'. Georgina, however, had been warned by the wronged wife of Fancourt, who has dressed as a Savoyard beggar to get her ear, of the danger from two men (Fancourt and Tippy) who plot her ruin. The two villains are exposed but Fancourt, the cad and bully, will wreak an awful revenge on his wife for alerting Georgina to his plot; but this is avoided because, in recognition of her saving Georgina's honour, she will become, on Georgina's marriage to the man she loves, Conway, 'mother, sister, friend' to Georgina under her father's roof.

The comic background is brilliantly done and entirely believable. Here Hannah had the enormous advantage of having been able to study at very close quarters the working of the local and Parliamentary election systems in her home town of Tiverton with all the attendant corruption, bribery, patronage and broken promises. Sir Robert, a typical victim of the system, is in no doubt that he should collect the reward for services rendered in Wales, 'I was for ever on horseback; there was not a cottager who could influence the sixteenth cousin of a voter, whom I did not entertain' ... but true to life, he shows the typical misgivings of upstarts and provincials, of the nouveau riche and country bumpkins when he is to receive Lord Beechgrove. He is in a frenzy of indecision. The scene is Sir Robert's library: 'Sir Robert (sits) No, I won't receive his Lordship sitting (rises), that will look like want of respect. I will be standing. No - that will not be the thing neither; for then I shall have no opportunity to shew my veneration by rising at his entrance. No - I must sit, and - Yes, there I've hit it - I'll be reading - deeply employed in reading. Then, when the great man enters, start up, and dash away the book. Let me see, it shall be a large book. I'll get up and reach one down (mounts the library steps, and takes down a book) - Chamber's Dictionary - that will do (takes down another). 'The Fall of the Roman Empire' - Bless me - my Lord!' In his haste to greet Fancourt who enters with Tippy (dressed as Lord Beechgrove), he tumbles with the books. They help him up.

Hannah would also herself have experienced the enthusiasm of Sir Robert's 'bubbly' young daughter, Georgina who is carried away by all the excitement of the London scene. She is especially enthralled by Lady Horatia Horton's studio. Lady Horatia is a leading woman sculptor, unusual even in London; to Georgina it is an exciting new pastime and Lady Horatia has encouraged her. Hannah makes the most of this, for women, novel form of self-expression. Georgina is in the studio, modelling Andromache, suitably robed when Tippy, this time posing as a connoisseur of art, comes in with Conway, who has fallen in love with Georgina. Tippy, claiming he has just returned from Italy with all its art treasures, sneeringly examines Lady Horatia's statues through a monocle, calling them the work of a 'block chopper'; but he over-reaches himself when, to illustrate how unlifelike the statues are, he catches hold of Georgina's real and living foot. She screams and Tippy is shown up as the complete fraud he is and quickly decamps.

Hannah's plays show a strong streak of patriotism and none more so than 'The Town Before You'. Young Sidney Asgill is deeply in love with the sculptress, Lady Horatia, but thinking himself too poor to ask for her hand, decides to join the navy. On receiving his uniform, he proclaims, 'In this dress ... what gallant acts have been achieved! Those who have worn it have given England all her glory, have given her the boundless empire of the ocean'. He continues in this strain, 'let us look with gratitude towards a Howe' ... and follows up with an invocation, 'I quit my country ... to serve her. O! May the boundless blessings of heaven descend upon her; may my arm contribute to restore peace to her; and may GLORY and MONARCHY be hers, till time shall be no more!' While he is aboard the *Victory* at Portsmouth, his philistine uncle visits and insults Horatia; 'My nephew in love with a stone-cutter! A hewer of marble! Why he may as well live in a quarry'. However, it becomes clear that Asgill will have means enough to marry Horatia and he returns to London. Patriotism is still the order of the day; in the play's closing speech Asgill confesses that 'the enthusiasm which seized me, when I trod the deck of the *Victory*, can never be chill'd' and ends on a splendid 'Mother of the Free' note, when (advancing) he declares, 'Ah! Repose on us! And when you look on the gallant spirits, who do honour to this habit (his uniform), let every fear subside; for, whilst the sea flows and English sailors are themselves, ENGLAND MUST BE THE

MISTRESS OF THE GLOBE!' This chauvinism seems overdone even by 'Land of Hope and Glory' standards, but it must be remembered that 'The Town Before You' was put on when England was up against a really powerful enemy in France; recently Howe's victory of the Glorious First of June, 1794, had vindicated England's claim to 'rule the waves'.

Hannah's patriotism should not lead one to suppose that, essentially, she was a died-in-the-wool, hard-line, upper-class supporter of the *status quo*. Far from it. Despite her father, Philip Parkhouse, having been educated at Blundell's School; despite his close friendship with Lord Harrowby's local intelligence officer, Beavis Wood, Town Clerk, who supplied his paymaster with weekly reports on the political affiliations of the 25 voters whose support would be paramount in the next election; despite her dedication of a play to Queen Charlotte and another to Lord Harrowby, Hannah was a free agent, a fearless and honest independent thinker in the true tradition of her native town.

This is illustrated by her subtly espousing the unpopular cause of women's rights and her humorous pen portraits of faulty practitioners in medicine, justice and education at the time. The very fact that she is recorded as one of the subscribers to Martin Dunsford's *Historical Memoirs of Tiverton* (1790) shows that she was not afraid to show support for a writer who was anathema to the establishment. Martin Dunsford was a prime mover in attempts to get a much less restricted voting system established in the 'rotten borough'. He was the leader of the 'Opposition', 'The Committee of Petitioners and Natural Rights Men', and as such posed a threat; his influence was based on the then seemingly minor office of churchwarden which he quickly made the focus of the advocates of reform. The radical view was not to be realised until the Reform Act of 1832 but Hannah could appreciate its validity; the closing years of her life in Tiverton were a clear sign of her liberal and humanitarian leanings.

XV
HANNAH RETURNS TO TIVERTON

Thomas Cowley died in 1797 at sea on a small vessel taking him to Calcutta to visit his only surviving daughter, Frances. She had married the Rev. David Brown, chosen Provost of the magnificent new college at Fort William, Calcutta; it was a prestigious appointment; the college was on a grand scale, with Professorships in Divinity, Law and Oriental Literature. The Library of Tippoo Sahib and his rich Museum, chiefly collected by his father Hyder Ali, had been placed there.

Apparently Thomas did not leave anything to Hannah in his will; this is hardly surprising in view of the distance and time involved in those days (a six months' sea voyage via the Cape). The part played by Thomas in Hannah's success as a dramatist is difficult to assess. He seems to have had a considerable flair for writing. When Lord Harrowby, Tiverton's former M.P., was soliciting advancement for Thomas, he was to some extent relying on Hannah's achievements. He wrote to a Mr Wheler:[15]

Mr Thomas Cowley is a lively active man of good character and he has a considerable command of language both in speaking and writing. He has a small place in a City office which he means to resign and he is going to India as a cadet, not it is apprehended from any difficulty of circumstances, but in the hope of making some provision for his family. His wife, Mrs. Hannah Cowley has distinguished herself much in the dramatic line, having been the author of a comedy called 'The Belle's Stratagem', and several other pieces which have been very well received and what is rather extraordinary in a female play-writer is a most excellent wife and mother.

Mr Cowley is between 30 and 40 and though he goes out as a cadet, it is by no means his wish to remain in that condition. He means to get it the moment he can obtain either a secretaryship for which he seems well qualified or any other tolerable civil situation, and if Mr Wheler can promote this by any application to his brother, it would be felt as an obligation by Lord Harrowby and he would assist a family of merit who have not at present so large a share of the good things of the world as they seemed entitled to.

In his own right, Thomas was well-known in literary circles. This was not always useful to Hannah. A much publicised review of 'The Belle's Stratagem' in *The Gazetteer* of 9 November 1780, criticised the 'tedious coldness and langour' of that season's production (the second for the play).

The reviewer complained of the intrusion of 'new jokes' more appropriate to the country than to the town and presumably introduced by the actors on their own initiative. In closing, he lamented that 'every author, unless he happens also to be a manager had perforce to accept such interpretations of their role, whether he thinks proper or not'. The outspoken critic of *The Gazetteer* was - Thomas Cowley!

Possibly Thomas was trying to be helpful to Hannah but in the event the reverse was the case. This review, understandably, did not go down at all well with the cast. However, on 21 November, the *British Mercury* reported that Mr Cowley and the actor, Mr Aiken, playing Saville, had 'resolved differences over the critique'. Not the end of the matter; Hannah herself was now involved. The theatrical gossip columnist, the 'Ear Wig' had heard that Mrs Cowley had written to several of the cast complaining of their performances. 'Ear Wig' attributed their neglect of proper attention to annoyance at *The Gazetteer* review and, according to him, Mrs Cowley's view was that 'Such retaliation, she thinks, is cruel; for the critic and the author should be considered as two different persons'.

One result of Hannah's retirement to the tightly-knit town of Tiverton, deplored by Professor Link, is her blue-pencilling of the earliest editions of her works in preparation for the 'Works' editions of 1812 and 1813. He gives as his reason for preferring the original texts, Hannah's many subsequent alterations such as the striking out of 'Sbud' (slang for Christ's blood); 'Till the world danced a jig like a top' became 'till the earth went gaily round under me'; a 'knotty' problem became an 'obscure' one. Presumably these changes were made by Hannah herself; back home again, she would find it only right to conform to local standards of propriety and she would have had time to recall some of the more unfair objections and demonstrations in the London theatre, for example the hostile reception of 'School for Greybeards' and 'A Day in Turkey'. From a playwright whose proud boast was that every character spoke in his or her own idiom (clearly one of Hannah's outstanding skills) this is indeed sad but she would not have wished to jeopardise her new-found role as a local 'do-gooder'; she never relinquished her compassion for the unfortunates of this world.

Hannah now had no reason to stay in London; the preface to her last play 'The Town Before You' had shown her disillusionment with the buffoonery and gimmicks which had invaded the theatre and no family ties kept her there. Her son, Thomas, who had become a lawyer had apparently gone to Portugal; Mary, her elder daughter had died and Frances was unlikely to return to England. Back home, in Tiverton, there had been changes but the Parkhouse bookshop and printing house founded by her father, Philip, was still in Fore Street. He had died in 1790 and Hannah's sister, Mary, now had charge of the family business; it was to continue in being until the late nineteenth century.

The war with France was hitting the town hard. The 'Tiverton Fencibles' were mobilised and drilled at the Works (the outworks of the Castle near the Lamb Inn); a troop of the Tiverton volunteer cavalry commanded by Mr Worth met on 10 July 1797 in splendid scarlet dress with gold lace, but in a comment reminiscent of 'Dad's Army', Col. Harding says 'not being fully appointed, they were provided with short sticks in lieu of swords.'[16] Two years later, the Lord Lieutenant issued a notice requesting the town of Tiverton to select competent 'Guides' mounted and armed who could 'unite the force of this country and prevent confusion in the case of invasion'; they too represented a kind of 'Home Guard'. By 1803, ' in consequence of the threatened invasion', the loyal inhabitants of Tiverton were called on to register their names stating what office they could fill for the public defence:

1. Bearing Arms when an enemy has landed
2. Pioneers
3. Guides
4. Engaging to supply waggons and carts
5. Millers to supply the Army
6. Bakers to do the same.

Periodically the militia were drafted in; in July 1799, no less than 600 of the South Devon force, under command of Lord Rolle. French prisoners-of-war on parole were quartered on householders; a curfew bell rang out from St George's each evening at 5 p.m. to remind them to

Tiverton Market Cross, near the Parkhouse bookshop, was removed to ease traffic in 1783.

return to their billets. Trade in wool and cloth had much slackened off and the price of bread and even of potatoes soared beyond the reach of the poor.

Otherwise, the familiar face of the venerable town which Hannah so loved was much the same apart from the handsome market cross which formerly stood in the middle of Fore Street not many yards from the bookshop and which had been removed in 1783. The great castle still dominated the high cliff above the River Exe and adjacent was that comforting symbol of happier times, the church of St Peter. This was the family church of the Parkhouses; here Hannah was baptised, and here was buried her elder daughter, Mary Elizabeth who died on 18 November 1789 while preparing to visit her father in the East Indies. As a Corporator Philip, on civic occasions, would have sat behind the Mayor's Pew with its colourful statues of the Lion and Unicorn, both rampant, on the Corporation benches.

Despite present troubles, there were reminders of a generous and caring town to comfort Tivertonians in these stressful times. The great House of St George, home of wool baron, George Slee, and the adjoining almshouses which he had built in memory of his 12-year-old daughter, Eleanor, who died in the great fire of 1598, still graced St Peter Street: across the Exe Bridge almshouses given by John Waldron still adjured passers-by to 'Depart thy goods whilst thou hast time, after thy death they are not thine. God sav Elizabeth'. In Gold Street, stood another legacy of the 'wool bonanza', the Greenway almshouses with their exhortation to 'Have grace ye men and ever pray for the souls of John and Jane Greenway'. As well as the almshouses, John Greenway had also given the outstandingly beautiful chantry chapel to St Peter's Church; on the exterior, sailing on realistic waves are the ships which carried his goods abroad, armed merchantmen well-equipped with cannon, for those, too, had been troublous times.

Unchanged were lovely 'Old' Blundells in tree-lined grounds above the Lowman, and in St Peter Street, the mullioned Chilcott School. Unchanged, too, were the inns, the Angel still welcoming travellers –

The Mayor's Pew, St Peter's Church.

not to mention thirsty Corporators from the Town House which was joined to it by an underground passage; the Three Tuns which played a vital part in the town's political and social history – not only did the Mayor and corporation and clubs such as the Humorous Categorical Society repair there on the slightest pretext, it was also the 'watering-hole' for Old Boys of Blundell's school: and finally, the historic White Horse where both Fairfax and Cromwell are reputed to have stayed.

Hannah wrote no more plays. Her concern with the injustices which beset women continued, however; for some years she held a working party for up to 40 ladies on a Monday morning and, a fitting close to a life devoted to highlighting the iniquities of the system which condemned many women to a miserable life with a totally unsuitable partner not of their own choosing, the proceeds were 'for the benefit of distressed married women'.

Hannah's status as a leading playwright and poet had made her socially much sought after; *The Gentleman's Magazine* of April 1809 in an obituary comments, 'In the different characters of daughter, wife, and mother, Mrs Cowley's conduct was indeed most exemplary. Her manners were lively and unassuming, her countenance was peculiarly animated and expressive ... the most incontrovertible proof that her manners were pleasing is the estimation in which her memory is held by all who had, in so many directions, the happiness of her acquaintance'. The 'Biographical Character' relates that she wrote two or three slight poems in the last ten years of her life 'in friendship with the families of Lady Carew, Lady Duntze (Sir John Duntze was one of Tiverton's two M.P.s from 1768-1795) and Mrs Wood.' Only two manuscripts remained with her at her death. One was her ironic commentary on an 'Elegy on Lord Nelson' by a local clergyman; 'Mercy, what Nelson's Ghost again!' she began. The other was, typically, in a good cause. A sexton of the parish had had his little cottage destroyed in one of the disastrous floods with which the Exe so regularly overwhelmed the town. Hannah wrote a poem describing the sexton's frantic efforts to save his little home and the consequences of losing it, and signed it 'A School Boy' as a pseudonym. The list of subscriptions began with that of 'The School Boy' and, according to the 'Biographical Character' quickly 'more than restored his property who was so soon to assist in the funeral of his benefactress'

Interestingly, a letter from Hannah to Richard Phillips dated 20 November 1801 shows that, given a specific assignment, she would have been happy to continue writing. Richard Phillips, founder of the *Leicester Herald*, a vehicle for his strong radical views (in 1793 he was imprisoned for eighteen months for having sold a copy of Paine's *Rights of Man!*) was a publisher in St. Paul's Churchyard where his monthly magazine and basic textbooks were enormously successful and he had clearly been in correspondence with Hannah about the possibility of some literary venture. Discussing possible projects, her letter to him gives an insight into her character which had changed little:

> Sir
> I should rather be employed on a lofty subject than a quiet one. I am not at ease on level ground - there is not exertion enough - I love to be impelled violently ... To tell you truth, I have been a little extravagant in my furniture and garden and I wish to be still further extravagant and wish to say to myself that I have a right to be so. You perceive at once then, that not only the pleasure of writing but the gold which may accompany it is in my view. Sordid as the Inspiration is, I will own no other - I will create a new Parnassus, and Plutus shall be my Apollo.[17]

There is no record of any further involvement with Mr Phillips who became a sheriff of London in 1807 and was knighted in 1808.

The garden Hannah speaks of ran down to the river Exe which makes it probable that she was living in either St. Andrew or St. Peter Street where the old houses fronting two of the ancient throughways of the town have steeply sloping gardens on the river bank. She was home again, back among the people who had inspired many of her characters, people like the Pendragons in 'Which is the Man?'; Hannah had them coming from Cornwall but their characters would ring just as true had she had them come from Tiverton. People like the Justice; as her father was one of the 'top 25' in Tiverton, i.e. those 'corporators' entitled to elect the two M.P.s, Hannah would have met several local dignitaries not concerned with dispensing justice to the small fry such as publicans needing a licence or poor families needing validation of residence to entitle them to poor law charity. The Justice (in 'The Runaway') ignores his mundane duties but is moved to action when he hears of an infringement of the poaching laws. People like Gradus (in 'Who's The Dupe?'), a pompous 'larnèd gentleman' for whom the prototype would have been provided locally by the academics of Blundell's School (founded 1604) or by the gentlemen who frequented her father's bookshop, and whom she would have met daily.

Hannah was buried in the churchyard of St. George's, the beautiful Georgian church designed by John James, the famous architect associated with Sir Christopher Wren. This was a comparatively new church; the foundation stone was laid on 1 December 1714 when it was feared that if restrictions on dissenters were reimposed on the death of Queen Anne, there simply would not be room enough in the ancient (1073) church of St Peter. In the event, with the accession of George I, the overflow did not materialise and St. George's church became 'redundant' and was used as a woollen goods store until finally the work went ahead and the church consecrated on 11 October 1733. That Hannah was not buried in St. Peter's is surprising; her father, Philip Parkhouse, had married her mother, Hannah Richards, there and it was clearly the family's church; (St. Peter's churchwarden's accounts show that in 1776 the bookseller was paid £6.3.6. for a new Bible, Testament and Prayer Book); the rest of the family are buried there.

It is entirely consistent with Hannah's independent turn of mind that she should have given thought to the spiritual leanings of both churches; she would, in all probability, have found St. George's more to her liberal

St George's Church where Hannah Cowley was buried in 1809.

tastes, less rooted in class structure and giving more emphasis than St. Peter's to the New Testament and the teachings of Christ and their application to the problems of the congregation. St. George's had always been regarded as the 'evangelical' church in a very radical-thinking town; a sort of half-way house between the hard-core non-conformists and the established 'traditional' church.

It is indeed sad that a broken piece of stone is all that Tiverton has to show to commemorate the town's only outstanding playwright. The reasons are not hard to seek; in an agricultural community, before the advent of machinery, the more hands to the plough and the scythe, the better. Tiverton as a male-oriented society has progressed slowly to some sort of 'fair-dos' for women. It was not until around 1990 that women were permitted to be full members of such local clubs as the 'Constitutional' (Conservative) and uproar broke out when it was realised that women would be genuine full members and have access to the billiards room! At the Tiverton Golf Club (whose patron and most distinguished member is the renowned woman golfer, Joyce, Lady Amory), women were certainly not welcomed on the same terms as men. They were restricted as to the hours and days when they were allowed to play and access to the bar was difficult.

Attitudes are changing, even in the small West Country town of Hannah's birth. Blundell's, for nearly 400 years a stronghold of exclusively male education, has welcomed the new climate of opinion and now admits girls from the age of 11. The result has been welcomed by parents, teachers, boys and girls alike.

In the long struggle for women to play a full and equal part in life, Hannah was one of the true pioneers. Professor Frederick Link of Nebraska University, an authority on Mrs Cowley, has put it clearly in his introduction to the last edition of her plays (Garland Publishing Inc. of New York); 'Her plays have also been forgotten, and the best of them are worth remembering ...' He judges that 'The Runaway', 'Which Is the Man?' and her last play, 'The Town Before You', might well have a claim on posterity but goes on to say that 'Who's the Dupe?' and 'The

Belle's Stratagem' are among the best of their kind. He concludes, 'Perhaps the successful revival of such plays as John O'Keefe's 'Wild Oats' (1791) will encourage producers and directors to look beyond the works of Goldsmith and Sheridan towards other viable plays of the period ... For after all, comedy does not belong in the histories of the drama only, but on the stage'.

REFERENCES

1   R.D.Blackmore, *Lorna Doone*, Chapter 1.
2   Lt. Col.Harding, *Historical Memoirs of Tiverton*, Appendix p.34
3   *Georgian Tiverton*, ed. John Bourne, Devon and Cornwall Record Society, Vol. 29 of new series, Introduction, p. xx. The book is based on the 25 volumes of Tiverton Pocket Borough Correspondence (1756-1843) held at the Harrowby MSS Trust, Sandon Hall, Stafford.
4   *Georgian Tiverton*, p.34. Beavis Wood to Nathaniel Ryder, 21.8.76
5   *The Gentleman's Magazine*, Vol. 53, 1783, p. 540
6   Harrowby MSS, letter ref. 155
7. Harrowby MSS, letter ref. 14
8. Preface to 'Albina'
9   Alan Kendall, *David Garrick: A Biography,* Harrap, p.160
10 Harding, Vol.2, Book IV, p.117
11 Gerald Barnett, *Richard and Maria Cosway*, West Country Books, 1995, p.117
12 Barnett, p.107
13 Rev. E.S.Chalk, *Notes and Queries (Devonshire Association)*, p.242
14 Chalk, p.243
15 Harrowby MSS, Vol 1163 (Tiverton IV) f. 101 b
16 Harding, Vol.1, Book 1, p.165
17 Unpublished letter from the collection of John Wild (Tiverton Museum)

INDEX